DeFi for the Diaspora

Creating the Foundation to a More Equitable and Sustainable Global
Black Economy Through Decentralized Finance

By

Kamal Hubbard, JD, CFE, CSX

Paperback ISBN: 978-1-7367097-0-2
Ebook ISBN: 978-1-7367097-1-9

First paperback edition February 2021.

Cover art by Tracey-Renee Hubbard

Dedications

To my wonderful wife Tracey-Renee. Thank you so much for your patience, constructive criticism, and support of me during my journey through the crypto rabbit hole. To my parents whom I owe debt of gratitude that the even the cryptocurrency market cap cannot pay back, thank you both for everything you sacrificed for me and encouraging me to be my best. My two older brothers for always looking out for me growing up and during adulthood. To Mary Ethel Hill and Vernice Tuggle for being there for me so many times throughout my life and sharing your wisdom, guidance, and protection.

Contents

Chapter 1

Bitcoin is a Zero-Sum Game

Theft and destruction of Black wealth is a common theme throughout modern history. Whether it was the massacre and decimation of Black Wall Street in Tulsa, Oklahoma where more than one thousand Black-owned homes and businesses were eradicated[1]; or the theft of tens of billions of rands by apartheid regime bankers, officials, and politicians from the South African people during Project Spear[2]. Another less egregious example of financial discrimination that disproportionately affected Black communities includes the practice of redlining, where banks routinely denied mortgages and home equity loans to prospective Black borrowers[3]. What is most shocking about redlining is that it was at one time approved by the U.S. Government, as well as the possibility that redlining still occurs today despite a federal ban[4]. Putting these illustrations together with figures that nearly 326 million adults in Africa are either unbanked or under-banked is simply staggering[5]. Recently, the argument that Bitcoin has the power to save Black people from these financial woes has been gaining traction.

It is worth admitting that Bitcoin has been an incredibly successful endeavor that has steadily brought blockchain and cryptocurrencies into mainstream discussion and debate. However, Bitcoin will not save Black Americans and the Diaspora due in large part to the fact that as a collective, we do not currently have the bandwidth to leverage the asset to address our needs as a whole. There are a group of people out there that feel differently. These people feel the accomplishments and dominance of Bitcoin is attributed to it representing the entirety of what an investor could want in a virtual currency. These people are called Bitcoin Maximalists[6]. Contrary to this popular belief, Bitcoin Maximalism also will not save Black America or the global African Diaspora. To be clear, I am not saying that it is not a good idea to have or hold Bitcoin, but it's not going to solve most of the financial problems that have historically plagued Black people. One reason I say this is back in 2018, at the beginning of the latest cryptocurrency market downturn that most dubbed "Crypto Winter," I worked on numerous large lot over-the-counter orders of Bitcoin. Most of these participants were big banks, hedge funds, private equity firms, family offices, and other financial institutions that saw the financial opportunity Bitcoin presented the year previously, during its all-time high, and were preparing for the next uptrend in the market. During the numerous negotiations that I was a part of, none of them discussed acquiring Bitcoin to alleviate the circumstances of the Black community or the poor and forsaken among us. Instead, over the last two years, financial institutions have been onboarding onto the Bitcoin network with the primary objective of increasing their profits and exerting control over this emerging technology and asset class. Big banks and other financial institutions have crafted some of the most predatory and discriminatory practices against our community, the continent of Africa, and the

Diaspora, and there is no indication of this changing now that these institutions are investing in Bitcoin.

The subprime mortgage crisis ushered in a global economic meltdown where very few were held accountable. Instead, financial institutions were deemed "too big to fail" and received bailouts, while people pursuing the dream of home ownership were kicked out of their houses and suffered financial ruin. Black Americans are still suffering from the aftermath of subprime loans, which has widened the gap between White and Black homeownership, greater than it was in 1968 when housing discrimination was legal[7]. Now banks are legally allowed to custody cryptocurrencies for their customers, signaling a major shift in the regulatory environment that has shunned digital assets ever since their inception[8]. If we put this up against years of unequal treatment from banks, do you really think banks will begin extending crypto-related services in an equitable manner to our community?

Another reason why Bitcoin is not a complete solution for the Black community is White supremacist views within the ranks of the Maximalist community that Black people should not spend time trying to appeal to or correct. In the wake of the extrajudicial police killing of George Floyd in June 2020, Nick Szabo retweeted a post on Twitter that attributes the "race problem" to "…scientifically-documented, and persistent differences in average IQ between racial groups that make it unsolvable[9]." Nick Szabo is a legal scholar and computer scientist who is credited with conceptualizing the smart contract, and who dons the Thin Blue Line/Blue Lives Matter flag on his Twitter account[10] [11]. This flag became the go-to replacement for the Confederate flag when NASCAR banned it from their events. This tweet does not take into account the racially biased history of the IQ test, but that aside, Nick Szabo is regarded by some Maximalists to be Satoshi Nakamoto, the creator of Bitcoin, so to see him espouse these beliefs is highly concerning[12]. Furthermore, Szabo has heavy sway in the governance of Bitcoin, and none of this governance to date has found a way to specifically make Black people's lives easier. White supremacists were driven to Bitcoin largely in 2016 and 2017 when their organizations were being booted from websites like GoFundMe, Patreon, and PayPal. Bitcoin's pseudo-anonymous nature appealed to many White supremacists due to the way they could use it without being publicly exposed for their support of these subversive organizations. During the latter part of 2017, they began to experience the secondary benefit of Bitcoin's market rise to its all-time high, thereby providing funding for their operations and support of their leaders. Alt-Right leader Richard Spencer tweeted, "Bitcoin is currency of the alt right." Andrew Anglin, the publisher of the *Daily Stormer*, a Neo-Nazi message board and news website, at one time was thought to have had access to as much as $25 million in Bitcoin[13]. Any further question of the White supremacist presence in Bitcoin should look no further than the @NeoNaziWallets account on Twitter for up-to-date tracking of White nationalists' funds moving on the Bitcoin Blockchain[14].

Weeks leading up to the deadly insurrection on the United States Capitol, a chronically ill White Supremacist from France sent nearly $525,000 in Bitcoin to fellow White Nationalists and online Alt-Right personalities and organizations in America before committing suicide. Laurent Bachelier, who went by the screenname "Pankakke," sent 28.15 in Bitcoin to 22 wallet addresses in one transaction to assist in elevating the recipients' respective online platforms and operations[15]. Pankakke had a history of spewing racist posts in Bitcoin message boards, such as declaring "Blacks are born to be slaves anyway" as far back as 2013[16]. In Bachelier's suicide note, he decried the decline of Western civilization and questioned whether George Floyd really died during his encounter with police, among other farfetched notions[17]. Pankakke's transaction taking place on December 8, 2020 included individual donees such as Patrick Casey, Vincent Reynouard, and Ethan Ralph[18]. Patrick Casey is the executive director of the American Identity Movement, formerly known as Identity Evropa, which is regarded as an alt right white supremacist group by the Anti-Defamation League[19] [20]. Vincent Reynouard is a French Neo-Nazi that has been imprisoned for denying the Holocaust[21]. Ethan Ralph is a self-proclaimed member of the alt-right that interviewed several White nationalists on his YouTube show before his account was suspended[22]. Organizational recipients included VDARE, Bitchute, the Daily Stormer, and American Renaissance[23]. The single largest beneficiary of Laurent Bachelier's transaction was Nicholas J. Fuentes, host of the America First livestream. Nick Fuentes attended the Unite the Right rally in Charlottesville and allegedly has made numerous racist and anti-Semitic statements such as denial of the Holocaust. He purportedly claimed that if a White woman were to have sex with a dog or a Black man that both would be considered "degenerate" acts[24] [25]. Throughout December of 2020, Fuentes endorsed the riot at the Capitol that turned deadly social media[26]. The night before the events at the Capitol, Fuentes advocated for the killing of legislators as part of the murderous "Stop the Steal" movement[27] [28]. Although Fuentes denies being present inside the for the storming of the Capitol, there is no denying that the funding of White supremacists via the Bitcoin blockchain has been taking place for years and as the price of the digital asset increases, so does the brazenness of their acts[29].

Something else to consider with Bitcoin is that the cryptocurrency has been used to facilitate some of the most abhorrent crime imaginable. One example of this was an undercover sting operation out of Italy that was launched in October of 2019 that saw the arrest of twenty-five suspects as part of an investigation into the torture, sexual assault, and murder of children[30]. The law enforcement effort named, "Operation Delirio[31]," discovered that two Italian teens paid Bitcoin to view these heinous acts. Text messaging between the two young people included descriptions and depictions executions, sex acts on animals, dismemberment including castration, and barbaric videos that involved Nazi imagery[32]. Although Bitcoin is used often in Deep and Dark Web transactions, it is important to appreciate that these types of activities are not what Bitcoin is primarily used for, and that crime carried out using government issued currencies far exceeds the crimes paid for with cryptocurrency. Nevertheless, how would you feel if the Bitcoin in your wallet was used to carry out an unspeakably despicable act? What if you were somehow implicated in another's criminal activity by way of a mistake that was made during forensic blockchain analysis? Black people are not wrongly accused of criminal activity all of the time but do make up the majority of unjust convictions that are later overturned, that is if a fair post-conviction review even takes place[33].

Bitcoin was only the beginning of something big. I give credit to the Bitcoin blockchain and the many Black people who adopted it early and have been able to profit from the cryptocurrency. This small group of people in our community has been able to think differently about this thing called money. However, if we are truly looking toward freedom from the current financial infrastructure and more fiscal autonomy and self-determination as a community, Bitcoin as it stands and where it is headed will not get us there.

The latest market rise is due in part to new people coming to the ecosystem, and Black people in particular are being targeted to buy Bitcoin. This raises a major issue in which banks and White supremacists who got in at the bottom of the last market downturn have an opportunity to severely damage the financial futures of Black Americans and Black people around the world. It is imperative to understand that the espoused philosophies regarding Bitcoin are a zero-sum game and why there are winners and losers. One way that this plays itself out is with the people who were able to enter the market early and exit at the detriment of those who showed up the latest. Furthermore, the game is structured where the uninitiated will be in the best position to lose. There is a lengthy track record in the value of deception and Black people are now being deceived into ignoring these facts for the sake of financial gain.

It is best to provide the background knowledge we should all have before moving forward seriously with Bitcoin and other cryptocurrencies.

Black Americans and the Diaspora need networks that are fast and scalable, where we have control over the technology, the governance, and a sizable stake in the consensus. The real opportunity lies in a special incarnation of decentralized finance. Decentralized finance or "DeFi," is one of the most promising new technologies to emerge out of blockchain technology in recent months that enables things like decentralized lending, borrowing, and money markets. DeFi gives the Diaspora the ability to create its own banks, issue its own loans, determine rules and terms of those obligations, underwrite insurance products, and much more.

This text is intended to be an approachable informational manual where you can move ahead or go back to chapters based on your understanding of basic finance, economics, blockchain, and digital assets. It is meant for people of all technical levels without being overly granular. Later in the book, I will flesh out a more in-depth roadmap of how we as a people can fully leverage decentralized finance and how we can expand our economic options. I hope this book can allow you to begin thinking differently about money in the digital age and how these assets have the power to create a paradigm shift for people of African descent in America and throughout the world.

Chapter 2

THE CHRONOLOGY OF CURRENCY

T he world moves based on the concept of money and how much faith we have in it. We need money to buy the goods and purchase the services required to sustain our lives. In this way, it is difficult to imagine life without it. Money is so important that a slight interference in the way it circulates can create a serious fiscal crisis that stalls everything, including businesses and government operations. We've seen this in the United States recently when COVID-19 caused businesses to close due to health concerns, and the government had to pass swift and sweeping regulations to keep money flowing throughout the economy to prevent a financial collapse. This event may have given way to the next step in the digital evolution of money as we move away from large scale use of paper money and physical coinage. Before we look to the future, it is important to examine past forms of currencies to best understand the situation we face now.

A World without Money – Barter & Trade

Money, in some form, became a part of human history in the past 3,000 years. The conundrum that money unravels is what is known as the "double coincidence of wants" or when two parties have goods or services, they are mutually content with exchanging with one another[34]. The economies that existed before this time involved the system of barter trading. Bartering is a direct trade of goods and services without any medium of exchange. For example, people could directly exchange livestock for grains. It also involved swapping goods for a service. For example, I give you a stone axe if you help me hunt an animal. However, there were a few problems with this form of trade because this sort of arrangement takes time. One would have to find a trading partner who needs what they are offering and has what they need. This partner must also be convinced that whatever good or service they provide is worth what they are receiving. If these two conditions were not met, the trade would be cancelled until someone else agreed with the deal. The process of trade in this system was slow. This breakdown in trading highlights the concepts of liquidity and mediums of exchange. Liquidity can be understood on many different scenarios, but chief among them is the availability of an asset to satisfy your most immediate needs and assets in surplus to account for unforeseen circumstances[35]. A medium of exchange is an object or a system that expedites the sale, purchase, or trade between parties[36].

The next phase was the progressive introduction of a prehistoric currency that involved easily traded items such as weapons, salt, and animal skins. These traded goods served as a medium of exchange; however, the value of these goods was still negotiable. The system of barter and trade was used across the globe. It has survived through centuries and is still being used in some parts of the world today.

The Use of Cutlery in Asia

Around 770 BC, the Chinese began moving away from using actual tools and weapons as a medium of exchange, and instead adopted the use of miniature replicas of those tools. The need to carry these replicas comfortably in a person's pocket demanded their modification. People did not want to injure themselves on sharp tiny objects such as daggers, spades, and hoes[37]. They started abandoning these objects for the less injurious shape of a circle. These new shapes began the history of using coins as a medium of exchange.

Historical Currencies in Africa

One of the most well-known examples of historical currencies in Africa is the Cowrie Shell. Their use as money predated metal coins and paper currency to make small and large purchases[38]. The shells were associated with fertility and were often strung together in the amount of 32 shells at a time, called a rotl[39]. Kissi pennies were thin iron rods that stretched between 12 to 15 inches long that were exchanged in the countries of Sierra Leone, Liberia, and Guinea[40]. They were flattened at the ends and wrapped together to increase their financial worth. Kissi pennies were thought of as having a soul, so if they happened to break, they would need to be taken to a blacksmith in order to revive the spirit of the Kissi penny[41]. Katanga Crosses were named after the Katanga region and used throughout central Africa to facilitate commerce and trade. The crosses were made from copper and sometimes repurposed for jewelry and coinage after transactions were made[42].

Coins and Currency

Minted coins were first created in Lydia (Western Turkey). The king, Alyattes, minted the first official currency in around 600 B.C[43]. The coins were made from a mixture of gold and silver that occurred naturally. They were stamped with pictures that gave the denomination value. These currencies helped Lydia to increase its internal and external trade. Minted coins helped the country become one of the richest empires in Asia Minor.

Paper Money

When it was thought that Lydia had taken a lead in the currency developments, China made a great comeback with paper money. They went ahead to dominate the development of paper money in the following decades. By the time Marco Polo visited the country in 1271 A.D., the emperor had established a good system and policies for handling both the money supply and various denominations. Back in Europe, people were still using coins up until the 16th century. The use of coins was supported by the acquisition of precious metals from coins that allowed the printing of more coins. The banks then began promoting the use of banknotes for users to carry around in place of coins[44]. The notes could be taken to banks at any time and exchanged for their face value in gold and silver coins[45]. The paper money operated much like today's currency. However, only banks and private institutions issued these currencies. The colonial governments in North America became the first European governments to issue the first paper currency. The shipment between Europe and the colonies would take long and the colonies would often run out of cash as operations expanded. To solve this issue, the colonial government introduced IOUs that traded as a currency. The first IOU was used in Canada[46].

The Gold Standard

As mentioned above, paper currency could be exchanged for precious metals like gold and silver. When a government's paper money is tied to the price of gold, their currency conforms to what is called the gold standard[47]. The gold standard allowed countries to establish a valuation of their currency based on the price that country's government determined for gold. This standard also formed a basis for which two countries could establish acceptance of each other's paper money and better facilitate trade. After several countries adopted the gold standard, it operated at its height from 1871 to 1914[48]. The gold standard began to crumble during the onset of World War I as the countries that had adopted the standard had new and different political alliances and agendas [49].

Bretton Woods System

In July 1944, in Bretton Woods, New Hampshire, the United Nations Monetary and Financial Conference was convened with emissaries from forty-four nations with the objective of establishing a new monetary system in the wake of World War II and the Great Depression[50]. During the period between World War I and World War II, countries began abandoning the gold standard due to competitive devaluations of gold and other factors that served to erode confidence in the precious metal, thereby affecting currency values[51]. Those in attendance at the Bretton

Woods conference sought to develop a monetary system that would avoid competitive devaluations, solidify exchange rate cohesion, and encourage economic growth[52]. Delegates of the forty-four countries came to an agreement that gold was the basis for the U.S. dollar and all other currencies were to be fixed to the value of the dollar[53]. The Bretton Woods conference also saw the creation of the International Monetary Fund and the World Bank[54]. The Bretton Woods System came to an end in 1971, when the inventory of US gold fell, raising the possibility that the gold supply may be incapable of covering the US dollars in circulation. This caused President Nixon to devalue the dollar, which prompted a run on gold reserves. In response to the runs, Nixon suspended the practice of exchanging dollars for gold, marking the beginning of the end of the Bretton Woods System[55].

Fiat Currency

After the Bretton Woods System, the United States and other countries adopted another system of paper currency that was issued by their governments that were not pegged to a specific commodity for their value[56]. These currencies are known as fiat currencies and are what most governments have in operation today. Fiat currencies derive their value from the governments that issue them and the parties that enter into transactions with a given country's fiat[57]. Since fiat is not tied to a commodity or redeemable, its value is subject to inflation and deflation. In the United States, the dollar serves as both fiat and legal tender to settle public and private debts[58].

Currency Markets

The European governments' shift to paper money leads to increased international trade. Bank and the ruling governments created the first currency market by introducing the buying of currencies from other nations. The stability of governments affected the value of their currencies and their ability to trade on the international market. The competition between countries gave rise to currency wars. The competing countries would try to affect the value of their competitor's currency in three ways. They would drive the currencies low to reduce the buying power of their enemies. Sometimes they would drive the value up and make the enemy's goods too expensive. In some cases, they would attempt to eliminate the currency of the competitor. Today, the exchange of foreign currencies (FOREX) exceeds "\$6,000,000,000,000 in daily traded volume[59]".

Mobile Payments and Virtual Currencies

The 21st century marks the rise of two disruptive forms of currencies – Mobile payments and virtual currencies. Mobile payment involves making payments for products and services using portable electronic devices such as tablets, cell phones, or smartphones. Services such as Apple Pay, Samsung Pay, and Alipay are utilizing this technology. M-Pesa is another example of a mobile phone-based money transfer service, payment, and micro-financing service. It was launched in Kenya by Vodafone Group Inc. and Safaricom in 2007[60]. It has since expanded to other countries including Egypt, South Africa, Romania, and Albania.

It allows users to transfer, deposit, withdraw money, and pay for goods and services.

It is with a demonstrably firm understanding of the history of money and within this active financial technology space that in 2009, Satoshi Nakamoto introduced the first virtual currency, Bitcoin. Bitcoin became the gold standard for virtual currencies. These currencies do not have physical coinage. Virtual currencies – sometimes referred to as cryptocurrencies or digital assets, offer the promise of lower transaction fees and faster transaction times compared to traditional online payment mechanisms[61]. Virtual currencies are also decentralized, unlike the centralized fiat currencies that are issued by a government or quasi-governmental organization.

Money in itself is nothing but an idea, however, it is not an illusion. It can take the form of a metal coin, a shell, a piece of paper with an image on it, ones and zeros, photons, etc. Money is very real because we want it and need it to be real. In other words, money is energy, and all that matters is the agreed value that people place upon it. This value has nothing to do with the physical value of money, which is clearly demonstrated through the value proposition of virtual currencies and digital assets. Money finds its value in being a medium of exchange, a storehouse for wealth, and a unit of measure. It allows people to trade goods and services indirectly. Money is only useful because of the mutual trust that people have placed upon it, thereby making it a useful form of payment.

Chapter 3

MONEY MARKETS AND EXCHANGES

There is a distinction between money and capital. While money is a medium of exchange, capital consists of all the goods in the world that are subject to sale or transfer. Naturally, the supply of capital is limited and the production and consumption of capital are recurrent. The excess of production over consumption is usually used as a new capital for the creation of additional production, which can lead to more income. The owner of this surplus production may decide to reinvest it back to production or transfer it to others. Money markets operate on this principle. For example, in a banking context, an individual who has excess money can deposit it in a bank. The bank then loans (transfers) the deposited funds to another individual with the immediate need of it for a fee for a specified period, known as interest. The individual in need of the money would then return the funds with interest after the agreed period, thereby allowing the bank to make a profit and the person who made the original deposit to earn interest on their money. In that case, money has been traded (used as a capital) rather than a mere medium of exchange.

A classical definition of an exchange is a marketplace where securities, currencies, commodities, derivatives, and other financial instruments are traded. The basic function of an exchange is to promote the smooth operation of an economy and ensure fair and organized trading. It also provides efficient circulation of price information for any instrument trading on that exchange. Exchanges provide a platform for governments, companies, and other groups to sell financial instruments to the investing public.

An exchange can be a physical location where traders meet to trade or an electronic platform. Exchanges are located in many countries globally. The most common exchanges include the New York Stock Exchange (NYSE), the Tokyo Stock Exchange (TSE), and the London Stock Exchange (LSE)[62].

Electronic Exchanges

Trading can also be conducted on electronic exchanges. It is no longer required of all members to be present on a centralized trading floor to conduct trade. There are sophisticated trading exchanges that ensure fair-trading even though members are geographically far apart. The floor of the NYSE processes less than 15% of the total volume of stocks traded.

Requirements for Listing

There are minimum listing requirements for any company or group that would wish to offer a security for trading. The requirements vary from one exchange to another, with some exchanges being more rigid than others. The basic requirements, however, include minimum capital requirements, regular financial reports, and audited earning reports. These requirements aim at protecting the traders. Similarly, FOREX exchanges choose which currencies to list based on demand and other factors, such as value.

Factors Affecting Prices in Exchanges

Demand and supply position is the basic factor affecting the prices in both stock exchange and FOREX rates. The exchange rates are the rate at which a currency may be converted into another. This value may fluctuate daily with the changing market forces of supply and demand of currencies from one country to another. Similarly, the shares with more demand will command a higher price. Additionally, exchange rates can be manipulated by governments to encourage imports by making imported goods less expensive by decreasing the supply of their currencies. Conversely, they can encourage exports by devaluing their native currency so that foreign currencies have more purchasing power for the goods they export. Here are some leading factors that influence the fluctuations in the exchange rates of currencies more so than stocks:

Inflation Rates

A change in market inflation causes a change in currency exchange rates[63]. A country whose economy experiences a lower inflation rate than other countries will experience an appreciation in the value of its currency. If the inflation rate is low, the impact on the prices of goods and services increases at a lower rate. A country with a consistently lower inflation rate exhibits a rising currency value. On the other hand, a country with a consistently higher inflation rate exhibits depreciation in its currency. Such countries are usually accompanied by higher interest rates. Regarding inflation, below are some historical examples of how inflation rates affected a country's currency value.

Weimar Republic

After its defeat in World War I and the signing of the Treaty of Versailles, the German government was reformed under the new name of the Weimar Republic for the period of 1919 to 1933. In the years following the war, the exchange rate of the mark (former German/Weimar Republic currency) began to markedly decrease. Redress payments as a consequence of the war, exfiltration of the nation's financial assets, the cessation of foreign trade, and a ballooning national debt all contributed to the decline in value of the currency[64]. In order to meet its obligations, the new nation began to create and circulate new money to satisfy their expenses. This resulted in out of control hyperinflation where the country's currency fell precipitously. Before 1914, 4.2 marks was equivalent to $1; by 1922, $1 could be exchanged for more than 7,000[65]. This currency decline continued through 1923 and was accelerated once the French occupied a portion of the then Weimar Republic, imposing crackdowns and blockades exponentially devaluing the exchange rate of the mark to 4,200,000,000,000 for every dollar.

This economic destruction led to political division, the evisceration of wages and the working class, food riots, and the commercial sector returning to the barter system for a period of time. Civil unrest persisted and the country was on the brink of civil war, then a new currency called the Retenmark was installed to institute some degree of economic stabilization. What made the Retenmark different was that it was restricted to a finite quantity and was backed by the manufacturing and agricultural assets of the country. The ending of money printing ushered in a more stable currency, which allowed the country to focus on the other unanswered issues such as tackling the war debt, increasing trade, and improving foreign policy. Sadly, as the economic situation began to turn the corner, the years of financial pain suffered by the people of Weimar sowed the seeds of political extremism leading to the rise of Adolph Hitler and the Nazi party taking power and starting the Second World War[66].

Zimbabwe

The first country in the twenty-first century to experience hyperinflation was Zimbabwe, which was originally subjugated under colonial rule by way of Cecil Rhodes through a royal charter granted to Rhodes' British South Africa Co[67]. The country was named Southern Rhodesia under the charter, and when colonial rule was winding down on the African continent in the early 1960s, Britain wanted Zimbabwe to be an independent nation that emerged as a multiracial coalition government[68]. However, much to the chagrin of the British Crown, the White supremacist Rhodesian Front party led by Ian Smith was able to win the 1962 election and declare independence from the colonial power in 1965, renaming the country Rhodesia. Smith spent much of his time in office refusing the Black majority of the country an opportunity for political participation and shutting down negotiations with Britain to the extent to where economic sanctions were imposed through the UN Security Council[69]. This White supremacist regime only strengthened the resolve of the Black majority to fight for liberation, and the Patriotic Front, led by Robert Mugabe and Joshua Nkomo, began staging guerilla warfare from bases in Zambia and Mozambique against the White minority government until a new constitution and transitional government took place in 1979. In 1980, Mugabe was made prime minister and the nation was officially renamed Zimbabwe; a coalition government was installed with Nkomo, and even Smith was able to take part in parliament[70].

The newly independent nation was off to a great start economically in 1980 with one Zimbabwean dollar (Z$) being worth more than the US dollar. In fact, the Z$ could be exchanged for $1.54 US dollars and real GDP was growing 14.6 percent over 1979's economic output statistics. In the 1990s, Mugabe sought to restructure the economics of the country as well as impose land reforms that would see to it that the land and resources of Zimbabwe be returned to those who preceded Cecil Rhodes. Many of the White farmers played a significant role in the country's economy through their agricultural operations signaled from their numbers when Mugabe came into office in 1980 with over 5,600 White commercial farmers[71]. The land reforms drove a decline in commercial farming that led to marked decrease in food production and unemployment. By 2009, there were just around 250 White commercial farmers still operating[72]. During the land reforms and government restructure, Zimbabwe began to experience higher rates of inflation and began printing higher denominations from the original Z$2 – Z$20 notes, increasing them to Z$50,000 and Z$100,000 by July of 2006. In early 2009, the largest note to ever be circulated was the one hundred trillion dollar bill (Z$100,000,000,000,000)!

The drop in food production made it difficult for farmers to obtain loans for agricultural growth, and other sectors in the economy also began to suffer to the point of the country's financial system collapsing. Additionally, Zimbabwe faced economic and other sanctions from the United States, the European Union, and the IMF[73]. The unemployment rate in 1982 was 10.8 percent and soared to 94 percent in 2009.

The combination of economic and political factors set the stage for out-of-control inflation; however, it was government spending in the face of these factors with no source of revenue that pushed inflation into free fall. One example of this was in 1997, when nearly 60,000 soldiers who fought against Rhodesian forces for Zimbabwe to be free, pressured the Mugabe government for pension payments that amounted to 3 percent of the nation's GDP for the year. Mugabe attempted to raise taxes, but the plan was rebuffed by the nation's trade unions, which induced the government to print more money to cover the cost of the pensions. This money printing persisted, and by 2008, inflation was over 231 million percent on a year-over-year basis. By 2009, Zimbabwe began to print a Z$100 trillion note. By this time, most people of the country had abandoned their native currency and opted for foreign currencies such as the US dollar, the Botswana Pula, and the South African Rand[74].

One thing that attracts people to Bitcoin is that it has a finite supply of 21 million coins. This means there will never be more than this initial supply and scarcity has been programmed into the system. Satoshi Nakamoto will not come out of hiding at some point to say he plans to increase the supply of Bitcoin to allow people another shot at obtaining them. So when you hear people regard the quest to have Bitcoin as a digital gold rush, there is something to this.

Interest Rates

Earlier in this chapter, there was an example discussing how a person deposits money with a bank and how the bank and the depositor earn a profit. The example illustrates the cost associated with borrowing capital or an asset, which is a simple definition interest[75]. To determine how much interest will be charged, sometimes this figure is stated by what is known as, "per annum." Per annum interest comes from the Latin translation of annually or each year[76]. A simple example of a per annum interest rate is a one-year loan on $100 at 10%, which require the borrower to pay $110 at the end of the one-year term. However, when dealing with a loan or investment, there are fees and expenses that are associated with the transaction that presented as an annual percentage rate or APR. APRs give the borrower or investor more of a total picture of what their interest will be once those fees and expenses are figured in[77]. Changes in interest rates are largely dependent upon central banks and the supply and demand of debt and credit in the marketplace[78]. A change in interest rate results in a change in currency value, exchange rate. FOREX rates, inflation rates, and interest rates are correlated. An increase in the interest rate causes the currency of the country to appreciate since a higher interest rate attracts more foreign capital. Bitcoin itself doesn't have an interest rate, however, many people recognize that this is still the early stages of adoption and the potential (and seemingly consistent) increase in price over time behaves as an extremely profitable interest rate although its simply appreciation of the asset and such appreciation will not last forever. Interest rates are also important in DeFi because they give a user an idea of how much to expect if they place funds with the protocol.

Political Stability

The political state and economic performance of a country can affect its currency strength. Such countries may see depreciation in the exchange rate. On the other hand, a country with fewer risks of political turmoil proves more attractive to foreign investors, thus drawing the investment away from other countries. More politically stable countries have less room for uncertainties in value of its currencies.

Egypt

In late 2010 and early 2011, Egypt and Tunisia were facing demonstrations against police brutality and government corruption and demanding ends to their respective dictatorships in what became to be known as the "Arab Spring." Heading into the Arab Spring, Egypt was experiencing expansions in GDP for the prior decade, some of the largest amounts of foreign direct investment seen in the country's history, and all time high levels of currency reserves equivalent to $37 billion. Despite this positive economic news for the country, poverty had risen along with GDP in the decade prior to the uprisings from 16.7% in 2000 to 21.6% in 2010[79].

Although it seemed counterintuitive for a country with economic growth on the macro level to encounter higher unemployment, it demonstrated that the corrupt officials at the top were not passing along those economic gains to the lower and middle class. Once average

Egyptians became fed up with this inequity, they took to Cairo's Tahrir Square seeking reform.

Hosni Mubarak spent almost thirty years presiding over Egypt's government and established an elite class that was able to experience financial stratification through the exploitation of his position[80]. As Mubarak was unseated, a military-backed government was installed to take over on a temporary basis until an election was held. Protestors shifted their demands for democracy from the longtime dictator to the troops who were now in charge but put forth a clear message that uncontrolled dissent would face a clampdown.

Egypt's majority party in parliament, the Muslim Brotherhood, waited in the wings for the election to take place to try their hand at administering democracy for the people. During this transitional period, new issues emerged in the absence of Mubarak's security forces like shortages in the availability of fuel, the marked increase of food prices, and instances of sexual violence against women[81].

This time of transition proved costly as the foreign reserves were exhausted by more than half after two years to $15.12 billion by April 2012 and had many considering if the currency would be devalued[82].

By July of 2012, the Muslim Brotherhood won a runoff vote with Mohamed Morsi, an engineer educated in the United States, becoming Egypt's fifth president. What made Morsi different from the other Egyptian heads of state was his lack of military affiliations, which created immediate discord with the generals set to hand over power[83].

In the promise of a new democracy, subsequent military and the Islamist governments at odds with one another faced challenges in balancing the economic scales towards the Egyptian people. Major concerns around crumbling infrastructure, lagging public administrations, expensive subsidies, and a confusing set of regulations made it difficult for the new governments to quickly impose improvements[84].

Instead of addressing the crumbling economy, Morsi spent the remainder of 2012 drafting a new constitution and attempting to win the power struggle with the military powers that saw him relieving many of them from their duties in the attempt to acquire more power. By early 2013, food prices continued to drastically increase, fuel and electricity were in short supply, the nation's birthrate was on the uptrend, and Egypt's long-term economic recovery was not coming together as the region and the rest of the world had hoped. The Egyptian people grew impatient with Morsi and began taking to the streets once again seeking change. In July of 2013, Morsi was deposed in a military coup that this time placed interim presidential powers in the hands of Egypt's Chief Justice of the Supreme Constitutional Court. Unrest continued through the end of 2013, and by January of 2014, the people of Egypt were set to vote on a referendum proposing another constitution[85].

The political instability of Egypt drove the economy down as it searched for democracy. The crisis caused inflation to rise to 14%, up considerably from 6% before 2011. To save itself from further economic peril, Egypt was seriously considering receiving a substantial financial aid package from the International Monetary Fund[86].

The Egyptian Pound (E£) was originally pegged to the prices of gold and silver then to the British Pound (GBP), until 1962 when the Central Bank of Egypt decided to change the value of the currency and pegged it to the US dollar[87]. The Pound lost 48% of its value by the end of 2016, and one of the terms of the IMF bailout was for the currency to untether itself from the US dollar in order for it to float freely on the currency markets. This stipulation was clearly a factor in the currency dropping further, leading up to the uncoupling of the two currencies but allowed for the much-needed injection of funds to address longstanding economic concerns[88].

Prior to this action, a US dollar was worth 8.8 pounds; however, once unpegged, a dollar was able to purchase 15 pounds. Since 2016, the Central Bank of Egypt has exercised measures to bolster the nation's economy and the Egyptian Pound. By April of 2018, the government had trimmed interest rates by 2% in an effort to attract domestic and foreign investment[89].

Political stability can apply to the cryptocurrency world in the way that a crypto or DeFi project at times comes at odds with itself due to external or internal politics. Miners may disagree with developers as to the future of the project, and this discord could have an impact on price until such factions come back to alignment. This has led to what some have described as "civil wars" in which the result is inevitably the creation of a new cryptocurrency whose principal value is that is similar to the original, but it prioritizes ideological values over financial value. The cryptocurrency you own is a statement as to the ideology represented by that network, which makes it important for each potential user to fully understand the world each cryptocurrency is looking to facilitate and make sure that it aligns with one's values.

Speculation

If traders expect the value of a certain country's currency to rise, they will demand more of that currency to make a profit when they supply it back in the near future. The increase in demand will lead to an increase in the currency value, which causes a rise in the exchange rate. The cryptocurrency market is highly regarded as a speculative market because everyone who invests in crypto projects expects for those projects to grow and appreciate. The process of speculation acknowledges the ideology represented by the cryptocurrency in question and risk of investment is then assessed as a function of how popular that ideology is perceived to be, or perceived that it will be in a given timeframe.

Mexico

Mexico in the 1980s faced what was known as the "lost decade" when the country underwent a debt crisis in 1982 and suffered heavily when oil prices toppled in 1986. When the early 1990s rolled around, Mexico was on track to turn the corner from the difficult economic trials faced in the prior decade. Foreign investment was coming in strong, interest rates were falling, and the Mexican central bank was stacking billions in reserves. To make things better, the North American Free Trade Agreement (NAFTA) was set to massively ease trade restrictions with Mexico's neighbor and biggest trade companion, the United States. NAFTA lifted the trade barriers between both countries in early 1994 in ways many thought would continue to invigorate Mexico's currency[90]. A myriad of issues arose that unraveled the positive steps of the Mexican government and its economy in 1994, which is another story unto itself, but Mexico's turnaround from the previous decade attracted foreign investment under the speculation of an appreciating peso. Speculation ties into a common adage around the cryptosphere of "buy the rumor, sell the news." The best way to act on this adage is to stay plugged into the community of a given cryptocurrency to catch early rumblings and read the pulse of a given project and make buy and sell decisions before you see people making these decisions based on the news.

Recession

Economies operate in a cyclical manner, known as the business cycle, where they experience highs and lows, expansions, and contractions. After an economy sees a period of growth, it will begin to decline; this decrease in activity is known as a recession[91]. Recessions cause interest rates to fall and decrease the chance of a country to acquire foreign capital. When the country cannot attract foreign capital, its exchange rate (price) will fall.

What better recession to highlight than the aptly named, "Great Recession" that occurred under the George W. Bush administration. The Great Recession is a pun of the "Great Depression" that took place after the stock market crash in 1929 and not fully ending until after World War II in 1946. During the Great Depression, the United States GDP fell more the 10% and unemployment soared to 25%. The policies of the Federal Reserve after a previous economic depression from 1920 to 1921 focusing on monetary expansion to stimulate the economy set the stage for the Great Depression. These measures included enlarging the money supply by $28 billion, which was a 61.8% increase from 1921 to 1928. This led to deposits at banks to grow by 51% and shares of savings and loan companies to swell by 224%. Where the Fed went wrong in this endeavor was that in 1917, it cut the required amount of reserve deposits to 3%, kept interest rates low, and failed to increase the amount of gold on hand by the US Treasury and itself commiserate to the expansionary policies. The accelerated growth and excess money boosted the real estate and stock markets to the point where the respective bubbles burst and the markets toppled in 1929[92].

Fast forwarding almost 70 years later after a not-so-great recession following a technology (dotcom) bubble and the attacks on the World Trade Center in 2001, the Federal Reserve sprang into action in the attempt to keep the economy steady. The tactic the Fed employed to do this was to lower interest rates drastically and suppresses rates from 2002 to 2004. Policies at the federal level seeking to preserve economic stability pushed a message of boosting homeownership. The mix of low rates and directives toward home buying ignited the financial and real estate markets, leading to a massive enlargement of the amount of total mortgage debt. Financial instruments were marketed that expanded the criteria of subprime mortgages, as well as the creation of adjustable-rate mortgages to entice borrowers that would traditionally not qualify on the understanding that rates would remain low. To the contrary, the Fed began raising interest rates from 2004 to 2006 to support a more balanced rate of inflation. The increased rates caused the amount of new credit entering the real estate market to decrease and served to raise the rates on the adjustable and variable rate of mortgage holders beyond what they bargained for when rates were at historic lows. This combination of events led the housing bubble to pop, ushering in a credit crisis in 2007 that was followed by the disintegration of Bear Stearns and the bankruptcy of Lehman Brothers, two of the United States' largest and most respected investment banks at the time. Once these two entities folded, a domino effect was set forth through the global economy with Europe feeling the brunt of the pain[93]. Black Americans that followed the message of homeownership promulgated by the government and banks may have suffered the most, in that by 2031, the average Black family will have $98,000 less than they would have if the Great Recession had not have occurred[94]. Towards the end of the Great Recession, around 8.7 million Americans were out of work as the unemployment rate was pushing at almost 10%; GDP fell 0.3% in 2008 and 2.8% in 2009; and consumer and household spending decreased as almost $19 trillion of net worth was lost on the stock market[95][96].

Crypto Winter

After the Initial Coin Offering (ICO) bubble of 2017, digital assets experienced a recession of their own in 2018 and 2019. 2017 was a year of growth with ICOs providing a launch pad for projects and serving as a means of expansion for the industry. Cryptoassets would see a major decline for much of 2018 and 2019. 2020 saw growth with renewed interest in Bitcoin and particularly when it came to decentralized financial protocols. Thus, cryptocurrency market capitalization is subject to the same cyclical nature present in any economy, however, in this case nobody really cared enough to term it as such and anyone who did care did not want to admit how bad it was.

Monetary & Fiscal Policies

Central banks can use policies to directly influence interest rates. Monetary policy is used by central banks to manage interest rates and the money supply[97]. One tool known as quantitative easing (QE) is utilized to increase the money supply by buying securities with the aim to lower interest rates[98]. The policies that influence the interest rates will determine whether investors will prefer to invest in that economy or not[99]. Monetary and fiscal policies demonstrate how governments and central banks can influence the economy in a given country, which is a major factor in the underlying value of a given fiat currency. Monetary policy, once again, is utilized by central banks to control the money supply and the interest rates, while fiscal policy focuses on taxing and spending[100].

QE Under Obama

Coming out of the Great Recession during the Barack Obama administration, the flagship fiscal policy took the form of the American Recovery and Reinvestment Act that saw the U.S. government undertake $831 billion in deficit spending, while the Fed commenced monetary policies that saw interest rates go almost to zero and delivered $7.7 trillion in emergency loans to banks through QE[101].

The American Recovery and Reinvestment Act (ARRA) sought to stimulate the economy through tax relief, infrastructure spending, heath care expansion, and investments in education[102]. QE occurs when a central bank buys securities off the market to buoy the money supply and foster lending and investment. The goal of Fed's QE effort after the Great Recession was to inject the banks with this money so that they could boost their lending and investing to increase overall economic activity[103].

Consternation began to form on two sides that were vehemently against the monetary and fiscal policies after the Great Recession. One side felt that the relief was too one-sided on the part of the banks and Wall Street; and the other side homed in on the fact that the Fed was essentially printing money ("money printer go brrrrr…"), which at some point was going to lead to inflation/stagflation and a massive devaluation of the U.S. dollar. Both of these sentiments played right into the hands of Bitcoin and cryptocurrencies in the way that if you felt like Wall Street caused the financial collapse that led to the Great Recession and you could no longer trust banks with your money, buying crypto served as a way out; conversely, if you felt like the government was printing money like it was nothing and that the value of those dollars would soon follow, you also bought into crypto. These arguments continue to resonate in a post-COVID-19 world with continued QE, the federal reserve deciding to begin purchasing exchange traded funds (ETFs), the Coronavirus economic stimulus and relief bills totaling over $3 trillion (CARES act, PPP, EIDL etc.), a national shortage of cash and coins, and even more of our consumer purchases taking place online; it should come as no surprise that there is renewed interest in cryptocurrencies once again in 2020[104]. Monetary and fiscal policies all played a role in the historical illustrations throughout the chapters to one extent or another. Regardless of which side of the argument you are on, if you are Black, statistically you more than likely suffered financially more than any other group after the Great Recession[105].

Exchanges and money markets are volatile since several factors affect the rates and prices of securities, currencies, and commodities. A trader must be up to date with these factors to evaluate the optimal time for buying or selling of a financial instrument or currency. Throughout much of this chapter, Gross Domestic Product (GDP) was mentioned. GDP can be looked upon as synonymous to a cryptocurrency project or DeFi protocol's output and real-world adoption beyond people buying and holding their coin. An example of this is whether people are bringing liquidity to the market, regardless of if it is through traditional market making or automated market making (AMM). Another example is if viable partnerships are being made where the use case of the blockchain a cryptocurrency represents is being used by businesses to improve their operations. Regardless, it is important to understand these underlying economic concepts and how they relate to tokenomics and the cryptoeconomy. The next chapter will cover more of the technical side of how all this works.

Chapter 4

BLOCKCHAIN

You may already be familiar with the term "blockchain," the record-keeping technology behind Bitcoin and other virtual currencies. Blockchain is also sometimes referred to as distributed ledger technology or DLT which is a distributed, decentralized ledger[106]. At the most basic level, "blocks" are digital information stored in a database where each record is "linked" to the next by unalterable cryptography referred to as "the chain." Blocks consist of digital pieces of information that occur in three parts secured by cryptography. The first type of data stored mentions information such as time, date, and the amount used in the transaction. The second type of information they store is about the people who participate in transactions, such as the payment address. The third type of stored information creates unique identifiers that allow certain blocks to be distinguished from one another.

What is Cryptography?

Cryptography allows two parties to communicate in secret in the presence of a third party that may want to eavesdrop on them. The two parties are able to encode and decode their messages through the use of what is called a cipher[107]. The cipher acts as an algorithm or set of steps allowing for the encoding and decoding of messages sent back and forth from one trusted party to the other. Applied cryptography secures a blockchain in the way that it uses the concepts developed to provide secrecy and repurposed by the blockchain to guarantee that any data being received is accurate, true, and the same as what was received by all other participants.[108]

How Does Blockchain Work?

Four conditions must be met to add a new block to the chain: First, a transaction must occur, in other words, someone must interact with the blockchain in a way that adds meaningful data. Second, the transaction must be verified which requires owning some of the cryptocurrency to create[109]. A network of computers verifies that the transaction happened in the manner that those involved in the transaction described through a process called consensus. Third, all transactions must be stored in a block. After a transaction has been verified to be accurate, the amount involved in the transaction and the digital signatures of both parties are stored in a block[110]. Fourth, the block must be given a cryptographic hash which is a unique, identifying code. The block is also given the hash of the most recent block added that "links" the chains together. Miners compete to be the first to properly construct a block of data which conforms to the rules of the network (called a "protocol") and are rewarded with more cryptocurrency for their efforts. The block can then be added to the blockchain once it has been hashed and the new block becomes available for people with access to view. For example, if you look at the Bitcoin's blockchain using an explorer, you will have access to transactional data and the information about when a transaction has occurred and for how much.

Blockchain is a decentralized system. This means that anyone can participate. No country, entity or individual will have their transaction rejected so long as it conforms to the established protocol. This is called a "permissionless system" as the only requirement to participate is to agree to follow the rules - and you can stop at any time. As mentioned, users can view the content, choose to connect their computer to the blockchain network, and become a participant by establishing what is called a node. In this case, you will be automatically receiving a copy of the blockchain that is updated whenever a new block is added[111]. Each computer in the network is granted a copy of the blockchain, which means that there are thousands or millions of copies of the same blockchain. Spreading the information about a blockchain makes its manipulation exceedingly difficult, and thereby establishing true decentralization. Successful manipulation of data stored in a blockchain would call for the manipulation of every copy in the network.

Are Blockchains Secure?

Blockchain takes care of the issues of security and trust in several ways. New blocks are stored linearly and chronologically. They are always added at the "end" of the blockchain. Therefore, each block has a position called "heights." After a block has been added to the blockchain, it is nearly impossible to go back and alter the content of the block[112]. Each block contains its hash along with that of the block before it. Hash values are created via cryptography that encodes digital information into a string of numbers and letters. An attempt to manipulate one block will cause a domino effect and will easily be detected. One example of an attempt to manipulate the blockchain is known as the double spend problem. Double spending takes place when someone tries to spend the same funds twice. This can occur because of a disparity in data or when a party to the transaction intentionally endeavors to conceal or misrepresent transactional data [113]. The process on how double spending is prevented is discussed more in depth in the next section discussing crypto mining.

One of the unique aspects of Bitcoin and other cryptocurrencies is their ability to make unified decisions in the presence of erroneous or otherwise corrupt data within the network known as the Byzantine fault tolerance[114]. Byzantine fault tolerance arises from a computer science concept known as the Byzantine Generals Problem[115]. This problem manifests when computers in different locations send data to one another in the face of glitches or malicious activity. In order for these computers to verify reliable data, they must all agree on data that is free of errors. Cryptocurrencies encourage nodes in the network to operate as honest brokers through the mining process to ensure the majority of nodes in the network agree on what data is true and which is false[116].

Crypto Mining

Earlier, the process of consensus was mentioned. Bitcoin uses a "consensus model" called proof of work (POW) to enable a computer that wants to add blocks to the chain. If a person wants to send crypto to another party, the sender will need their private key and the wallet address of the party in which they intend to send the crypto. The private key allows a wallet holder access to their funds. Once the funds are sent, a transaction is created that may be batched with other transactions that will then need to be verified to make up a block[117]. In the execution of proof of work, a computer must prove that they have done the work of solving a complex math problem. If a computer manages to solve one of those math problems first, then they are eligible to add a block to the blockchain and receive a reward in the process[118]. This process is referred to as "mining" because of the computational effort involved to capture the block reward and how the process serves to create new coins for the ecosystem. To check the transactions, mining computers are automated to select pending transactions from a pool, and to ensure that the sender's account is liquid enough to complete the transaction. The mining computer checks the transaction details and the history stored on the blockchain to avoid the double spend problem. It is followed by a second check to confirm that it is the sender who authorized the transaction with their private key. If the private key does not match, then the transaction is treated as fraud, and does not go through.

The next most common way of achieving consensus on a blockchain is called proof of stake (PoS). Although similar to proof of work in that it utilizes an algorithm to validate transactions, proof of stake operates differently by rewarding the creator of a new block based upon how large their holdings are of the coin being mined[119]. Explained another way, the coin holder with the larger stake in the network, or larger wallet, receives a larger block reward. Proof of stake is also regarded as being more environmentally friendly since it does not rely on the use of application specific integrated circuits (ASICs) that proof of work requires to capture a block reward. ASICs get their namesake from being strictly dedicated to mining Bitcoin and other cryptocurrencies relying on POW, which requires a considerable amount of ASIC units and electricity to operate[120].

Centralization vs. Decentralization & Distribution

The concept of centralization and decentralization are relatively easy to juxtapose. Centralization is present when information, authority, governance, and other aspects all reside in one place. An example of this is an enterprising business with a dedicated data center. Although the business may be spread out in different locations, those various locations link to the servers within that dedicated data warehouse[121]. Decentralization occurs when data, network control, computing power, etc. are spread out through different regions with no one node that has control or precedence over another. Examples of this are peer-to-peer networks like Bitcoin and Web 3.0 applications known as decentralized applications or "dApps." Under the distributed framework, the components of a system are scattered in different locations and coordinate with each other to make decisions in a centralized manner[122]. Examples of this distributed structure are content distribution networks, cloud computing, or a large internet company like Google[123].

Public vs. Private vs. Permissioned

Blockchains can be customized in a number of ways to meet the needs of its users. Depending on the use case of a blockchain, the content stored on it may either be open to the public, privately-held, or a hybrid of the two. The data on public blockchains can be accessed by anyone looking to join the network and viewed by utilizing a blockchain explorer online that will allow someone to view wallets and transactions taking place on the network. Private blockchains are just that, a distributed ledger that grants access to trusted and verified users to the data held on the blockchain. Although the private blockchain is distributed across a particular network, it is not truly decentralized because only a select group of people determine who has access and who can benefit from interacting with that blockchain. Permissioned blockchains are able to be configured to have aspects of both public and private blockchains[124].

Wallets

A cryptocurrency wallet allows users to send and receive funds to one another[125]. It can be looked at as the equivalent of an online digital asset account. They consist of a string of numbers and letters that require the holder to have a private key in order to access their funds. Since this random string of letters and numbers has no association with the name of a given user, sometimes people think that cryptocurrency wallets are anonymous. In actuality, cryptocurrency wallets are pseudo-anonymous, because all it takes is one item of identifying data tied to a user's wallet to be able to make an identification of that user. This is a good thing to keep in mind because in most cases, a user's interactions with their wallet can be viewed and tracked.

There are four kinds of wallets that a person can employ to hold their digital assets. Paper wallets allow someone to go online, create a new wallet address and accompanying key. If created and stored properly, paper wallets are thought of as among the most secure form of cryptocurrency wallet around. One major thing to keep in mind is if the wallet gets destroyed or lost without being backed up, the funds will be lost forever[126]. Web wallets are accessed online and hosted by a third party on their servers. These wallets are safe as long as the user and the third-party maintain sound cybersecurity protocols[127]. Software wallets are the type you can download to a local device, such as a desktop, laptop, or mobile device. This way, none of the information has to interact with the internet, making it ostensibly more secure than the web wallet option[128]. Hardware wallets are advantageous because they are more durable than paper wallets and can operate offline in the same way as software wallets. However, similar to paper wallets, if they are lost or destroyed, there may not be a way to recover the funds unless a backup has been generated[129].

Blockchain & Digital Coins

Putting things that have been discussed so far into context, the primary goal of blockchain is to allow the recording and distribution of digital information while preventing the editing of such information. In the Bitcoin whitepaper, Bitcoin is referred to as, "a new electronic cash system that is fully peer-to-peer, with no need for a trusted third party[130]." Fiat currencies such as the U.S. dollar are regulated and verified by a central authority, usually a government or a bank. In a central authority system, the user's data and currency are at the mercy of that central government, making the value of their money at risk[131]. This along with the economic collapse in the wake of the subprime mortgage crisis is among the challenges that inspired the introduction of Bitcoin. Since Bitcoin is built on a blockchain that is a decentralized network, it operates without the need for a central authority. This model reduces risk, eliminates many of the processing and transaction fees, and improves the speed of the transaction. Due to their decentralized nature, digital currencies also give people a more stable currency to rely upon if they reside in a country with an unstable currency, like Venezuela[132]. Bitcoin is groundbreaking, as it solves many of the challenges facing the fiat currencies. Digital currencies promote transparency, reduce the time and cost of transactions, and can promote stability against inflation and other factors affecting the traditional currency exchange market. For the above reasons, this technology has revolutionized the financial industry. However, as mentioned during the introduction of this book, Bitcoin is just the beginning...

Chapter 5

CRYPTOCURRENCY

From the previous chapter, blockchain technology and its usefulness in contemporary business and finance was discussed. Blockchain is a technology that not only inspires innovation like Bitcoin but also enables the existence of cryptocurrency. In this chapter, we take a closer look at the overall digital asset landscape.

What is Cryptocurrency?

One constantly posed question from those seeking information about crypto is how to make money from this whole new world of digital currencies. The best lesson to learn for newcomers to this technology and asset class is: Rule #1- there are no chargebacks! It is important keep this in mind as you move through the rest of this book and your own journey with digital assets to ensure you don't get burned or what you may hear in this subculture as "rekt." It is always the user's responsibility to do their own research on the coins they seek to possess to know the inherent risks posed by a particular digital asset.

Let's quickly recap (again); virtual currencies are internet-based assets that use cryptography to ensure security and no counterfeiting or double-spending takes place when conducting financial transactions across distributed ledgers. Cryptocurrencies leverage blockchain technology to gain decentralization, transparency, and immutability. However, the most important feature that differentiates cryptocurrency from fiat is that it is not controlled by any central authority, which is principally the decentralization feature it possesses. The fact that cryptocurrencies are decentralized theoretically protects it from government control or interference, as opposed to how it happens with the government issued and controlled fiat currencies. Said another way, cryptocurrencies are digital or electronic peer-to-peer currencies. From a tangible perspective, cryptocurrencies don't physically exist. In other words, no one can claim to have picked a Bitcoin in his or her hand, neither can anyone say they withdrew a material Bitcoin from an ATM around their block. However, just because you can't physically get hold of virtual currencies does not mean they do not exist in any other form or it doesn't have value. Cryptocurrencies' growth would not have been this phenomenal if it had no worth in the minds and hearts of so many. One question to ponder before moving forward is, what gives cryptocurrencies their value?

How Many Cryptocurrencies Are There?

While Bitcoin was the first breakout cryptocurrency, many have emerged to serve different purposes and use cases in the global economy. At the time of the publishing of this book, there were just over 6,200 cryptocurrencies valued at over 350 billion dollars, according to Coingecko.com[133]. The ballooning number of digital assets in the cryptomarket is an indication of a low barrier of entry for digital currencies. All you need is time, a minimal amount of capital, and a team that understands how to write computer code to develop your own cryptocurrency. The expectation is that the number of cryptocurrencies and the global valuation will only continue to increase in the future.

One of the reasons cryptocurrencies, like Bitcoin, were developed was to fix what many considered to be flaws with how money is transmitted from one party to another. Some of the most cited flaws with the centralized fiat currencies were delays in transactions and the cost of transactions. In regard to the delay, what is most arduous is the time it takes to complete transactions given the involvement of third-party financial intermediaries such as banks, particularly in facilitating cross–border payments. Furthermore, financial intermediaries have made transaction fees so expensive to the point of being considered predatory. Cryptocurrencies, therefore, work around these challenges to ensure the costs of transactions are not only low but fast.

Like fiat currencies, cryptocurrencies can be sent between two parties and used to buy goods and services. However, cryptocurrencies are much less expensive because of minimal processing fees that allow users to avoid the exorbitant fees charged by the mainstream financial institutions. This new system that provides opportunities for secure payments online through digital tokens, cryptocurrencies have become a global phenomenon that is gaining popularity every day. However, crypto as a medium of exchange is not what has propelled it to its current heights. Instead, it is interest in these decentralized and sometimes unregulated currencies in market trading that allows people to profit much in the way FOREX's fiat currencies trade. Since cryptocurrencies are decentralized and for the most part unregulated, sometimes speculators' activities make the digital currencies' prices extremely volatile, and it is within this volatility that presents the opportunity to make money.

Is Crypto A Good Investment?

The buying of crypto for speculation has been on the rise, and it is what has made digital currencies popular. However, skeptical investors at best see crypto as merely speculative and not real investments; at worst they see crypto as an outright scam. The reasoning behind this is like other traditional forms of currencies like fiat, cryptocurrencies generate no cash flow, which means someone has to pay more for the currency than you did for you to make a profit. The speculation of cryptocurrency relies on "The Greater Fool Theory" of investment, which simply means you buy some assets or securities hoping that someone somewhere will be willing to pay more at a later date. This is where classic "pump and dump" schemes have played themselves out in markets for years and is still highly prevalent in crypto. This also reinforces the notion that Bitcoin and other cryptocurrencies are a zero-sum game.

Contrary to this theory is a well-managed business whose value increases over time by the growth of cash flow. For cryptocurrencies such as Bitcoin to flourish, they need some form of stability. The stability will be good for the merchants and consumers, particularly in determining the fair price of goods and services. The reality is that cryptocurrencies have been anything but stable since digital currencies were founded. Let's examine an example of a small business that is experiencing growth in the year of 2016, and in 2017 decides to invest and incorporate Bitcoin into its operations. On January 1, 2017, the business buys 1 Bitcoin for $1,000, and over the course of four months spends part of the Bitcoin with a group of vendors who accepts it and sells the rest on the open market for a profit. By May 1, 2017, the business owner has seen Bitcoin grow by fifty percent and decides to buy another Bitcoin, this time at $1,500. By September 1, 2017, the market is only getting hotter and the price of Bitcoin is just shy of $5,000. Why not buy and sell another? By the time December rolls around, the price of a Bitcoin has peaked at slightly under $20,000. What a difference a year makes. 2018 is only going to get better, as it is possible Bitcoin could shoot to $100,000. So the business decides to leverage its assets and buy not just one Bitcoin, but three for $58,996.17 on Friday, December 15, 2017. Over the course of the next month, Bitcoin gradually declined, and by February 5, 2018, the business decided to sell the three Bitcoin valued at $20,556, which was sold at a major loss.

This illustration exhibits the extreme volatility of Bitcoin during a run up in price and a precipitous price dump. The decline was so sudden that those who invested for the short term counted serious losses. A small business that integrated it into their operations even with serious fiscal discipline would suffer greatly by this drop in price. This price volatility creates a sort of conundrum, which makes it difficult to balance itself in the market as hoarding would take effect among those who own the currency. Why would a person spend or sell their coins if the price could rise by say three times the value the following year?

Nevertheless, crypto is still a good investment when taking certain variables into consideration. One variable to examine carefully is the use case of the digital asset in which you are seeking to make a position. Will the use case of the coin/blockchain/project allow you or the average person to use that cryptocurrency to somehow benefit your life in real time? If that digital asset cannot help you now, what is the long-term outlook for its use? Will it be able to assist people and businesses in a not-too-distant future or are you willing to wait years if necessary, before experiencing a profit? Another aspect to examine is the team involved. Does this team have a proven track record of success and execution? Can they bring their whitepaper or business plan to life using the blockchain? When these questions are answered and placed in proximity with a market environment where buyers and sellers can determine price, you then have a better understanding of what gives cryptocurrencies their value. These variables aside, are you knowledgably able to trade in and out of these assets to mitigate your risk in the face of price swings? If you can confidently answer these questions, crypto is a good investment to consider.

So now that one of the questions posed earlier in this chapter has been answered, it is time to give you another tip when it comes to crypto investing. Remember Rule #1, there are no chargebacks! Sure, it sounds simple, and much has changed in the space to create safeguards for investors in crypto over the last few years, but to make this concept even easier to understand there are no refunds in crypto. There is no customer service hotline you can call once you have sent your coins to someone guaranteeing you a fraudulent 1000% return if you allow them to hold your coins for a week. If you send your coins to the wrong address, you cannot ask the wrongful recipient to give them back. It is important to be mindful of where you are sending your funds because there are slews of people out there that are trying to separate you from your coins. Keep this in mind, as it is by far one of most powerful maxims to hold onto if you want to make money investing in digital assets. Only trade with trusted individuals and established platforms; otherwise, it is caveat emptor!

Chapter 6

ALTCOINS & ICOs

Altcoins

If you are getting into the cryptocurrency market, you will encounter the terms "altcoins" or simply "alts" throughout your journey. In this chapter, I will explain what altcoins are, how to understand their features, how they are birthed through ICOs, and how they work in the larger crypto market. Any cryptocurrency that is not Bitcoin is considered an altcoin. The term "altcoin" emerged when other developers ventured into developing alternative cryptocurrencies after the Bitcoin breakthrough. The term altcoin is an abbreviation of "alternative coin," as in an alternative to Bitcoin, and it includes all those cryptocurrencies that came after the successful launching of Bitcoin. Today, there are about 6,200 altcoins in the market[134]. While some provide unique features, others are simply duplicates of Bitcoin attempting either to improve on the proposition of the number one cryptocurrency in the world or ride its coat tails. The leading altcoins are Ethereum (ETH), Tether (USDT), Ripple (XRP), Bitcoin Cash (BCH), Cardano(ADA), Tezos (XTZ), and ChainLink (LINK) among many others.

As just mentioned, when the motivation behind some altcoins is to attempt to create better or different versions of the Bitcoin, the goal is to develop something that would solve some specific weaknesses of Bitcoin. The developers of Litecoin created their currency to solve the problem of speed on the Bitcoin network, with much faster confirmation times. Tether was created to bring more stability when it comes to trading in the crypto world. Dash, Zcash, and Monero, on the other hand, were created to address privacy issues that Bitcoin is seen as failing to observe. Speed, stability, and privacy are all issues to consider before using Bitcoin. Although each altcoin claims to provide some unique functionality from Bitcoin and others, most have a lot of similarities with each other. Altcoins are also different from Bitcoin on how they are extracted, which provides a different perspective particularly when it comes to the mining process. The difference in mining algorithms means that most of the altcoins require different types of mining hardware and resource requirements. New altcoins often find it hard to penetrate the market because buyers and sellers often shun them unless they have some specific features that are extraordinarily unique. New coins suffer even more because they tend to have fewer wallets and exchanges supporting them. The trend explains why despite thousands of altcoins being released into the market, just a few have managed to make a mark in the crypto market, or even offer worthy competition to Bitcoin.

Initial Coin Offering

The initial public offering (IPO) is a common term in the financial sector, which signifies the point when a private company lists shares on a stock market and "goes public," rather than selling some of its shares to a select group of people to raise capital[135]. Initial coin offerings or ICOs are derived from this concept. Another term used loosely to describe an ICO, is a token generation event (TGE). The idea ICOs work in such a way that an investor is presented with a project, and if they are convinced that the project will succeed then they can invest. Once the project is successful, the investor may resell their coins for a profit. A crypto company launches a new project through an ICO by developing a whitepaper. A whitepaper is a document that provides information about the direction of the company or project, including its goals, missions, and visions. In other words, the whitepaper simply explains the project details, including the necessities, how much money they target to raise, the amount of coins the team plans to offer, and the conditions of the ICO among other factors.

The public is alerted to start investing once the ICO has been established and are directed to the ICO website. The investors can receive tokens in exchange for their money invested. The ICO works in such a way that if the money raised does not meet the minimum target set up in the whitepaper, called a soft cap, the company refunds investors their money. Inversely, if the company raises the maximum funds requested by the public, the ICO has reached its "hard cap" and they will cease collecting funds. ICO fraud is a subset of cryptocurrency fraud that cannot be overlooked. There are a number of ways ICO fraud can play out. The classic case is a fraudster sees the ICO as a way to raise millions of dollars and separate investors from their money. Other ways ICOs can become compromised is if the smart contract or the ICO website gets hacked. Some of these instances are actually inside jobs to take the attention off the team promoting the ICO. ICOs are no doubt a risky endeavor, but that's why crypto investors like them. There are many people who have experienced great success investing in altcoins through an ICO. However, for every altcoin mega success realized by someone, there are several projects that have turned out to underperform or be an outright fraud.

Chapter 7

THE REGULATORY ENVIRONMENT OF CRYPTOCURRENCIES

A major concern among investors is the regulatory framework of crypto and whether or not investing in cryptocurrencies and ICOs are legal. The state of regulation constantly remains in flux as blockchain technology continues to come to the forefront. For years, lawmakers were determined to associate Bitcoin and other cryptocurrencies with crime and criminals. However, if you examine how well represented the banking and finance lobby is in the United States Congress, it does not seem illogical that cryptocurrencies would receive such harsh treatment until they are able to establish more control over the industry. There is no denying the fact that Bitcoin and other altcoins were utilized by users of Silk Road and the dark web for a number of nefarious activities, but if you put into perspective the activities of the dark web vs. criminal activities paid for with US dollars, there is no comparison that more crime is paid for with fiat than with digital currencies. The good thing about cryptocurrencies when it comes to fighting crime is that since they operate essentially on top of a digital ledger, parties to a crime and other clues will be recorded on the blockchain. In this way, blockchain acts more of a deterrent than a facilitator of illicit activity.

Draconian measures by some governments have led to all out bans of cryptocurrencies, while they scramble to measure the threat cryptocurrencies pose to central, commercial, and retail banks[136]. On the other hand, several countries have embraced digital currencies and the innovation of distributed ledger technology by welcoming blockchain based firms to their shores and taking a hands-off approach to cryptocurrencies[137]. Three states at one point contemplated whether to let their citizens pay their taxes in Bitcoin with the State of Ohio approving the measure[138]. Adoption of cryptocurrencies is increasing in the United States, and more lobbying dollars are finding their way to Congress and state capitals around the country from crypto-related special interests. Hopefully, this infusion of lobbying dollars leads to more sensible regulation, because looking globally, the United States lags behind other nations that have acted quickly to provide legal guidance to its citizens and allowed blockchain technology companies to scale without the legal and regulatory uncertainty that drains money from the compliance budgets of blockchain companies.

In February of 2020, Securities and Exchange Commissioner Hester Peirce delivered a speech outlining safe harbor provisions for decentralized projects to raise funds for their projects. In the speech entitled, "Running on Empty: A Proposal to Fill the Gap Between Regulation and Decentralization," Commissioner Peirce recognized the confusion and lack of clarity digital asset developers face in attempting to raise funds to launch their projects, while attempting to adhere to the letter of the law[139]. The speech laid out the current issues faced by some blockchain businesses before asserting the proposal for safe harbor. It is important to understand that this speech opened the door to further innovation in the United States and provided guidance around ICOs and TGEs[140]. In the aftermath of the 2017 ICO craze, the Securities and Exchange Commission (SEC) vigorously lodged enforcement actions against a multitude of offenders who perpetrated fraudulent projects to investors. Such enforcement actions left good actors in a quandary of what to do next with limited resources[141].

A considerable issue holding up United States based crypto projects wanting to remain compliant in the face of launching their token was the Howey Test. The landmark case of Securities and Exchange Commission v. W.J. Howey in 1946[142], was a US Supreme Court case that established a legal test to determine if an investment is a security, thereby making subject to securities disclosure and registration requirements[143]. Reliance on the Howey Test raises the possibility that a company would have to spend a considerable amount of capital on registering and disclosing, which only brought about further confusion and consternation for the companies, regulatory experts and entrepreneurs alike. Commissioner Peirce's proposal would allow for a three-year period for projects to tokenize and adequately decentralize. During this three year period, the token or coin would not be deemed a security by the SEC, lifting a significant burden on those who were unclear how to navigate the previously murky regulatory waters. It is important to know that this proposed rule (Proposed Securities Act Rule 195 – Time-limited Exemption for tokens) will not immediately become a law or statute but does likely indicate the direction of the agency in the future when dealing with ICOs[144]. This proposal shows that the SEC is taking measured steps towards lessoning and clarifying regulation without stifling continued innovation and economic opportunity, which surely serves as a relief for many US-based crypto projects seeking funding for tokens.

Chapter 8

CRYPTO MARKETS

E arlier we discussed the concepts of markets and exchanges. When a person buys cryptocurrencies via an exchange, they buy the coins based on the underlying value of that asset. You can go long or short, depending on how you think the price will move. Going "long" simply means you buy if you believe the price will rise in value over time. Going "short" implies that you sell if you believe the price will fall. When a person trades on crypto price movements to sell or buy for profit, they are engaging in price speculation, enabling them to participate in the hope that a chosen digital asset will move in price so they can capture that profit. At the time of this book being published, there are close to 420 crypto exchanges according to www.coingecko.com, the majority of which are centralized. Most of the existing exchanges have their own learning curves associated with them that require a user to understand some basics in the user interface technology and the ability to understand charts to make use of the information they provide. However, once you find an exchange that trades the assets you like and aggregates data the way that best suits your needs, the more a user tends to stick with that platform.

How Do Cryptocurrency Markets Work?

Over the counter (OTC) trading takes place when a buyer and a seller contact each other to trade outside of a centralized or decentralized exchange in a peer-to-peer manner. OTC trading allows sellers to make a profit without being glued to a screen for hours conducting analysis of charts. OTC trading can be challenging, risky, and not very profitable, unless you are trading in large quantities. The difficulty of trading in large quantities can range from security issues to not coming to an agreement on the terms of trade.

Centralized Exchanges

Centralized cryptocurrency exchanges function more like traditional stock markets. They are owned and operated by individuals or companies with total control over all the transactions. They require a user to create an account, send assets to the trading platform, which therein takes custody of those assets or coins, while the person trades. The central controlling party of the exchange must identify the users through a process called, Know Your Customer, or "KYC." The user will be able to open a position by putting up the full value of the asset, trade across assets and experience price movements without immediately taking ownership of the underlying coins. Users on such platforms lack the permission for accessing the private keys of their exchange account's wallets. When finished, the user is able to transfer their coins and tokens back to their own wallet for safe keeping or trading on other platforms. Another type of exchange that is gaining in popularity is the decentralized exchange, which allows you to trade without releasing custody or possession of your coins. Decentralized exchanges will be discussed later in this book. Centralized exchanges are responsible for protecting user data and their trading information. They experience the same challenges as the stock market and any other centralized system. Sometimes they have privacy issues, and like any other website, they are prone to hacking. In 2016, Bitfinex was hacked and 119,756 BTC were stolen[145]. In the same year, Bitstamp was also hacked and 18,866 BTC were lost.

Factors Affecting Cryptocurrency Markets

Crypto markets are moved by many factors, most notably is supply and demand for digital assets. However, the decentralization factor tends to shield crypto markets from traditional economic and political factors that affect traditional currency markets. Nevertheless, there is still a lot of uncertainty surrounding cryptocurrencies, and it is important to highlight a few factors that may have a significant impact on crypto prices:

❖ **Supply:** when crypto is mined, there are a limited number of coins allowed in the market. Supply, therefore, means the total number of coins and the rate at which they are released, destroyed, or lost.

❖ **Market capitalization (Market Cap):** This is the total value of all the coins in the market, and the perception concerning its development.

❖ **Press and public information:** the portrayal of a digital asset in the media and the amount of coverage it receives can affect its price, demand, and acceptability.

❖ **Integration with the existing infrastructure:** if crypto easily integrates into any existing infrastructure, such as that of eCommerce payment systems, its values automatically shoots up.

❖ **Major events:** sometimes major events take place, including regulatory updates, security breaches, and economic setbacks in the larger economic environment that can affect crypto prices.

Looking at the crypto markets closely, you can always see to it that there is very little difference with other traditional currencies, except for the fact that the former is decentralized.

Trading on the Cryptocurrency Market

Trading on crypto markets is no different from other traditional markets, which involves selling and buying prices respectively. Often referred to as the spread, these are the prices quoted for a cryptocurrency for buyers and sellers. For someone who wants to open a long position, they are expected to check the buying price, which is slightly above the market price. When a person wants to open a short position, they are presented with the selling price, which is slightly below the market price. Trades take place on what is referred to as a "lot"; this is where the tokens trading are done in batches to standardize the size of trades. Due to the high volatility associated with cryptocurrencies, lots tend to be very small. This means that they are mostly just one unit of the base cryptocurrency.

Chapter 9

DECENTRALIZED EXCHANGES

(DEXs)

Aprimary reason that inspired the development of blockchain is to deal with the problems that come with centralized systems. Bureaucracy, slow speed of transactions, high transaction costs, and insecurity are some of the components that threaten centralized exchanges. It was the need to overcome these shortcomings that called for the introduction of decentralized cryptocurrency exchanges (DEXs). Cryptocurrency exchanges play a key role in the adoption and development of blockchain projects through cryptocurrency trading. The exchanges form a platform that connects the users to buy, sell, and trade opportunities. As someone looking to understand crypto trading and investing better, it is important to understand the difference between these exchanges and the impact it may have on your trading experience.

What is a Decentralized Exchange (DEX)?

A decentralized exchange system allows the users to carry out direct cryptocurrency transactions among themselves. They do not depend on a centralized exchange to keep their coins, provide private keys to complete transactions, or to offer security for the traders' coins. These exchanges, in contrast to the centralized exchanges, are managed automatically with the involvement of platform participants in the process of making important decisions. As a user, a DEX will allow you to interact directly with other participants. They use a distributed registry to store and process all data. A DEX does not store your funds or personal data on its server. It only serves as a platform for finding matches to buy and sell orders.

What Difference Does DEX Bring to the Industry?

Most of the strengths of decentralized exchanges spring from its distributed architecture and the lack of a single control center. DEXs solve the problems that are inherent in centralized exchanges by eliminating the third-party risk that comes by trusting one party to protect the data and funds of the users. When a person uses a DEX to trade, they are responsible for keeping funds and securing their data. This system spreads the risk, ostensibly improving user safety[146]. DEXs also present a low risk of price manipulation or falsification of trade volumes. Sometimes, centralized entities are interested in the manipulation inside their exchanges for profit-oriented reasons. DEXs also protect the exchange from the interference by local or international authorities[147]. For the time being, they are independent of regulators. If you are using a DEX, you are also capable of accessing different projects that may or may not be listed on centralized exchanges. Apart from allowing a trader to place orders for existing assets, DEXs also allow startup projects to list their assets and provide minimal liquidity, without having to incur the high cost of being listed on major centralized platforms. This distributed architecture of DEXs brings with it a few difficulties. The challenges include scalability issues, a small set of options, low liquidity, limited speed, and lack of technical support.

Can an Exchange Be Fully Decentralized?

Some existing DEXs that tout being decentralized are not fully decentralized in the first place. Many DEXs use their servers to store trading data and applications for the purchase or sale of user assets; however, the private keys are left in the hand of the users to keep and manage. DEXs have centralized components that make it possible to have some control over how they operate. A good example is the IDEX exchange, which prohibits New York State's residents from trading on the platform. Some of the exchanges may even be subject to hacking and attacks due to a similar reason. Examples of this are the EtherDelta decentralized exchange hack that took place in December of 2017, when 308 Ethereum were stolen, valued at over $250,000[148]; and the Bancor decentralized exchange, which was hacked on July 9, 2018, resulting in a loss of $13.5 million worth of assets[149]. An exchange can only be said to be fully decentralized when it cannot lose or freeze the account of the users. Currently, most DEXs have not reached that level. DEXs are groundbreaking technology, and they are a step in the direction towards zero-trust trading. However, there is still a much work to be done to optimize its application in the cryptocurrency industry. For the time being, one must deal with the challenges it comes with, especially the security, scalability, and liquidity issues.

Chapter 10

DECENTRALIZED FINANCE (DEFI)

The legacy global financial system still holds a firm grip on the world's economy. However, it has some inherent challenges that make it inefficient in certain aspects. Similar to the centralized exchange, the challenges that this system brings stems from its centralized structure. The major players, such as banks, hold unassailable authority within the industry. Today, if you are dealing with the bank, you will have to seek approval for nearly everything from getting a mortgage to making daily transactions.

This system also presents many intermediaries, which lead to numerous security issues. High reconciliation and administrative costs are also challenges associated with centralized architecture in the current financial industry setting. The global banking sector spends around $100 billion annually on the post-trade settlement and clearing securities within the developed capital markets[150]. The settlement of most securities still takes two days after the trade date, which leads to additional credit and market risks. The data of the consumers are also at risk when held by large central authorities. Meeting the consumer's expectation for fast and convenient digital banking processes is also a challenge.

Bureaucracy, once again, is another obstacle in this system. If you live in a certain zip code, have a criminal record, work a certain type of job, own a certain type of business, or any other reason someone with authority in the traditional banking system does not feel you are worth of credit; you will not have a loan extended to you. There is a long history of traditional financial systems engaging in practices that have shut Black Americans out of economic opportunities that would lead to community empowerment and financial sustainability. In searching for a solution to these challenges, attention is slowly turning to the blockchain industry that is capable of introducing decentralization in this industry. The primary goal is to make financial services accessible on a global scale in a swift, inexpensive, and secure manner. Another benefit that comes along with this is the shifting of trust from the bureaucrats, intermediaries, their performance, and their policies to the underlying technology and protocols that do not rely on centralization to offer the same services. The spread of decentralized financial services is creating a new financial frontier – Decentralized Finance (DeFi). At the DNA of DeFi is a decentralized architecture with blockchain at its foundation. This financial environment is characterized by faster settlements that eliminate unnecessary intermediaries and promise safe transactions.

What Does DeFi Look Like?

DeFi has a couple of characteristics that give it a distinct advantage over any centralized financial system. First, blockchain is open, meaning anyone anywhere across the world can access it[151]. Such a level of openness will solve the problem of inequality that is inherent in the current legacy financial system because all a person needs to engage these services is an internet connection. Second, the records kept in DeFi protocols are also scattered across many devices. No central server or body of authority has indomitable powers over the entire system. Therefore, this system is more secure since the attackers have no central target. Also, if you are a user and someone manages to get their hands on your data, it will be rendered useless without you. The chances of fraud and identity theft are greatly reduced in this system. As people are becoming the center of their data system through control of their identities, the business risk of larger data breaches is also reduced[152].

The current DeFi ecosystem enables things like decentralized exchanges (DEXs), decentralized stablecoins, decentralized money markets, decentralized synthetics, and decentralized insurance. All of these solutions have the possibility of reviving the concept of Black Wall Street and expanding it on a global scale that can't be destroyed as it was in Tulsa in 1921. Combine these solutions with other industries powered by blockchain and you can track, trace, and measure a global Black economy that has the ability to transact virtually instantaneously in a trustless fashion. As adoption continues to grow, it is imperative that Black people in the United States and the global African Diaspora leverage this technology in order to avoid the past predatory predicaments that currently plague us today.

Trust vs. Trustless

Earlier the concept of trust was mentioned, but now that the idea of the size and scale of what is at stake has been properly prefaced, it is important to elaborate on this further. An example of trust is that of a benefit check. A person trusts that the government or some centralized entity will cut and process a check, so that person can go to the bank and have it cashed. Those benefit checks show up every month or every regular interval based once again on someone trusting the government to put the check in the mail. In a trustless system, the decentralized framework of interoperating systems is incentivized to act in a certain fashion[153]. Thus, the reliance on a single centralized actor or a bureaucrat is no longer required. This essentially brings on the notion of which many within the cryptocurrency community regard as "programmable money."

Smart Contracts

Expanding on the concept of a trustless environment, it is important to touch upon smart contracts. A smart contract is a self-executing contract with the terms of the agreement between the two parties written within the lines of code. The code and agreement exist as part of a distributed, decentralized, blockchain network. The code controls the execution and the transactions are viewable on the blockchain in case a dispute arises[154]. In this way, smart contracts are able remove the reliance of trust by the parties involved in a transaction.

An example of a conventional contract would be if you ask your neighbor to paint your fence on Saturday for $250. In this scenario, you are trusting that your neighbor will come on Saturday with their paint, brushes, and supplies to do the job; and in return, your neighbor trusts that you will pay them once the job is finished. There is trust on both sides that your neighbor will live up to their word and that you will have the money once the job is done. However, in a smart contract scenario, you could hypothetically place cryptocurrency in escrow or within a smart contract and wait for anyone to paint your fence. Once the fence is painted in a satisfactory manner and that party is able to provide verification or proof of completion, the funds will be automatically transferred to them.

Decentralized Autonomous Organization

A Decentralized Autonomous Organization (DAO) is an intricate framework of smart contracts that can be used to reduce human errors and interaction to the point to which all essential and non-essential tasks are automated[155]. This network of smart contracts operates like bylaws and standard operating procedures that are programmed on the blockchain for transparency and to avoid arbitrary decision making. DAOs have the ability to make sure everyone is essentially operating in good faith by taking the human elements of greed and irrationality out of certain processes; and if something does go wrong, then the code can be analyzed to see where adjustments can be made, and the code can be patched to address previous shortfalls.

Decentralized Money Markets

In legacy finance, a money market is a place where savers, lenders, and borrowers come together for the purposes of bestowing money upon one another. Once again, a centralized authority determines the specifics of the terms, like interest rates, etc. Under decentralized money markets, there is no centralized authority to hamper these decisions. Instead, the key difference with decentralized money markets is that the assets are cryptocurrencies with smart contracts relegating the terms of the loans and interest rates. One of the biggest draws to DeFi is the fact that interest rates on crypto savings are more attractive than in conventional finance. All savers need to do is lock in their crypto onto the decentralized banking platform and allow their interest to accrue[156].

Collateralized Debt Positions

When it comes to lending and borrowing in DeFi, it is possible to get a loan almost instantaneously. You may be wondering, "how is it possible that someone is able to get a loan online without an ID, a credit score/credit check, or any other information on the borrower?" For simplicity purposes, a decentralized financial platform acts as a reserve bank that locks multiple digital assets as collateral to issue loans. These assets represent the collateralized debt positions (CDPs) for the various borrowers in the ecosystem. On an individual borrower level, a person will need to pledge digital assets that they already own as collateral for a loan of more cryptocurrencies to be paid back at a specified interest rate. If you do not repay the loan, the collateral pledged will be liquidated by the decentralized reserve bank. Thus, it is important to be sure to pay the loan back according to its terms[157].

Decentralized Governance

As governance has been mentioned a few times already in this text, it is important to define it and give it clear meaning as to how it fits into blockchain, cryptocurrencies, and DeFi. Governance is the decision-making process for a given entity or project that determines who is authorized to make decisions on behalf of an organization and how that process will be executed. Banks and other financial institutions from time to time will have their board of directors or shareholders vote on the future of these institutions. This process is centralized and reserved for specific individuals who have been chosen to be on the board or have the money to own shares of the bank. Decentralized governance removes this level of privilege and allows anyone who holds the digital asset, known as a governance token representing the decentralized financial protocol, to vote on the policies of that entity to affect upcoming propositions. Examples of the things that are voted upon include: adding a new collateral type, adding new risk parameters (new debt ceiling, liquidation ratios, stability fee, liquidation penalty, etc.), changing the savings rates, system upgrades, and other initiatives. The reason why governance is important is because governance for a permissioned blockchain may not necessarily be appropriate for a permissionless blockchain. Also, governance for a public blockchain seeking to serve a business purpose may not work for a use case seeking to meet the needs of citizens offering their contribution to the administration of public policy. So governance plays a vital role in shaping the future of a project and how stakeholders can make their voices heard. Some of the most important attributes of good governance across the board is that they have versatility and the ability to be upgraded when new circumstances arise[158].

Another advantage of decentralized governance is that it is powered by blockchain technology, which once again promotes complete transparency since transaction records are publicly auditable. Manipulating such a system is a tall order since it requires altering all the copies in all the computers within that network. This system boosts trust, which is imperative to handling financial issues. Imagine if the traditional banking system had to operate in an open and transparent way. If that were the case, there is a strong likelihood banks would operate in a far more equitable manner with its customer base. Thus, governance is an extremely important concept to understand because if it is properly harnessed, it can have a tremendous impact on improving the interests of the global Black collective by giving us a say in the financial issues that matter most to us.

Yield Farming

As mentioned in the previous section, in order to participate in the governance of a protocol, governance tokens are issued to DeFi platform participants. Another reason for the issuance of these tokens is to attract users to a particular protocol[159]. The process of earning governance tokens is as follows: an earned interest rate is assigned to certain assets when users decide to lend, borrow, or save their assets on a particular platform. In addition to the interest that a user earns or has to pay back for participating on that decentralized protocol, they also earn governance tokens proportional to the assets they utilize. This is yield farming in its most simplistic form, but the real objective of yield farming is to extend this ability to earn interest across multiple and multiple governance tokens[160]. To explain this concept further, let's say you save a digital asset, we'll say Ethereum for the sake of illustration; on Platform A for their governance token (GTA). Platform B will allow you to earn its governance token (GTB) when you offer liquidity on its protocol using GTA at a high rate of interest. In this way, Platform A users are enticed to join Platform B since they are incentivized by the notion of earning more governance tokens (GTB) from another governance token (GTA) that is earning interest on the Ethereum that was originally pledged on Platform A.

Decentralized Stablecoins

Stablecoins exist in digital asset trading to counter the volatility risk associated with cryptocurrencies. The value of a stablecoin is fixed or pegged to a real-world asset with far less volatility, like a currency or a commodity. Stablecoins can run into problems mainly attributable to lack of transparency. Two examples are if they are not properly collateralized and if there is not a trusted custodial partner managing the stable assets. The first example occurs if an entity says they have minted one billion dollars of a stablecoin, but the actual amount of money sitting in the bank is twenty-five million. This first example leads to the second, because a centralized stablecoin requires a trusted custodial partner to impose strict auditing and controls to maintain an accurate supply of the stablecoin to match the level of transparency blockchain can offer, or else, how can people trust that the asset is truly stable?

Decentralized stablecoins are much less susceptible to custodial risk because they do not have to rely upon a third-party entity for issuance, control, and governance. Furthermore, on-chain transactional history provides the transparency traders are accustomed to with all other cryptocurrencies. The different types of decentralized stablecoins include elastic-supply, collateralized debt positions (CDPs), self-collateralized, bond-redemption, single-currency, and multi-currency[161]. Regardless of the composition of the stablecoin, they have an important and valuable place in the cryptosphere by allowing for hedging against market volatility. As the ecosystem grows, there will no doubt be more decentralized stablecoin options available for DeFi participants.

Decentralized Insurance

The global insurance market was valued at over $5 trillion dollars in 2017[162]. Much of the value of this market in the United States and Europe can be attributed to the growth during the 19th Century for the underwriting of slave policies and related coverage[163]. This aside, in many cases, it is difficult for the average person to understand how the insurance works. Sure, it is easy to be sold a policy, but are you paying a fair price for a premium? How will you know if insurance will actually pay out if a triggering event takes place?

There are complex algorithms and considerations that go into the insurance industry, but with that said, there also appears to be a tremendous opportunity in bringing in blockchain technology and smart contracts to reduce trust in the system. As of now, the main use of decentralized insurance is to cover risk in DeFi loan products. The three main types of risks that exist in DeFi: financial, technical, and procedural. Users submit to the financial risk of investing into cryptocurrencies as a class of assets, and this risk is no different from any investment outside of virtual currencies. Cryptocurrencies and other investments are subject to market volatility, and as much as we would like the investments we buy into to significantly appreciate, there is the chance that they can lose all of their value. Technical risks arise if there is a bug or an oversight in the coding of a smart contract that makes it susceptible to being hacked or otherwise compromised. Another technical risk that can arise is if there is vulnerability within the hardware as opposed to the software. Procedural risks occur when users might be manipulated into using the platform in unintended ways (social engineering, phishing, etc.) that could lead to compromising the platform[164]. These are the risks that threaten DeFi lending, and in order to cover these funds, decentralized insurance policies are sold to protect users against things like digital asset downside risk and volatility, market flash crashes, hedging, stablecoin deposit protection, etc[165].

The decentralized insurance marketplace is ripe to expand with existing open-source predictive analytics suites coming to maturity coupled with the transparency blockchain can bring to perspective policyholders. Leveraging these predictive analytics to events that are particularized to Black people can serve as a measure to close certain gaps in coverage. New types of policies can be crafted away from the traditional insurance system that will give Black people the peace of mind to know what their premiums are going toward and have a solid expectation in how they will pay out. In this way, the possibility for decentralized insurance has a solid growth trajectory for Black people throughout the world.

Decentralized Derivatives (Synthetics)

Conventional derivatives can be described as a financial security with a value that is reliant upon, or derived from, an underlying asset or group of assets. The derivative itself is a contract between two parties with its price derived from market changes on the underlying asset[166]. The value of the global derivatives market is estimated at over $1 quadrillion dollars (>**$1,000,000,000,000,000**)[167]. Examples of derivatives include options contracts, futures contracts, and swaps[168]. The purpose of decentralized derivatives, also known as synthetics, is to allow users to gain exposure to an asset they want to trade without actually owning the underlying asset. Many synthetics derive their value mainly from other cryptocurrencies[169].

Where Are We Today?

DeFi is already a hotbed of innovation in the financial industry. Emerging markets such as the Philippines are already making the DeFi application a reality. The Philippines has some of the highest numbers of the unbanked population with 75% of the individuals in the country that are unbanked. Five million Filipinos (10% of the population) are already using cryptocurrency exchanges and applications to complete their daily transactions including paying utility bills. Colombia also presents a similar trend[170]. Countries battling with runaway inflation are also seeing rays of hope in blockchain technology. Venezuela, for example, is turning to digital currencies as a store of value at a time when they are battling with hyperinflation that has destroyed the value of their currency[171].

What does the Future Hold?

Cryptocurrencies and blockchain are on the path to revolutionize the financial system. More companies are adopting this technology[172]. Central banks across the world are taking up the research concerning the principles of cryptocurrency[173]. Some countries such as China, Sweden, and Uruguay are already down the path to digital currency adoption with a stream of new legislations and clear commitments; and as mentioned in the beginning of the book, the United States Congress threw around the idea of creating a digital dollar to expedite COVID-19 stimulus payments to citizens[174]. As we begin to consider cryptocurrencies in a broader manner towards economic emancipation, it is important to avoid threats that pose a risk of thwarting or derailing our efforts for greater economic freedom.

Chapter 11

PLAY AT YOUR OWN RISK

2020 was a year that demonstrated proof of concept when it came to DeFi; however, a number of mistakes were made along the way that are worth mentioning in addition to a broader discussion of the risks involved. In the last chapter, risk was touched upon in the context of decentralized insurance. However, total ecosystem risk is much more comprehensive than what can be covered by a decentralized policy. The three main risks present in DeFi are financial, technical, and procedural. Other financial risks include market risk, credit risk, and liquidity risk. Other non-financial risks involve issues with scalability, smart contracts, regulation, centrality, oracles, financial literacy, and of course the risk of future risks[175]. As much as it is important to know and understand the risks involved, it is equally important to illustrate how some of these risks played themselves out during 2020.

Black Thursday

Maker DAO is one of crypto's oldest DeFi protocols that provides a decentralized money market as well as allows users to mint the DAI decentralized stablecoin through pledging Ethereum as collateral. In

March of 2020, a 50% drop in the price of Ethereum brought about the under-collateralization of DAI, further causing the liquidation of tens of thousands of ETH through Maker's auction system[176]. A major contributing factor to the liquidation was the network congestion taking place on the Ethereum blockchain as people were attempting to exit their positions as well as those attempting to capitalize. In fact, the individual who capitalized the most was the lone bidder that was able to win 62,843 ETH for a miniscule amount of DAI via 1,461 auctions. This major loss sent users through the roof and straight to court where a $30 million class action case was filed[177].

The network congestion leading to this event was a classic result of scalability risk. Scalability risks occur when gas prices are too high or transactions on the blockchain are not able to be verified in a timely manner. The matter with scalability was so severe that some consider Black Thursday to be a type of Black Swan event. A Black Swan type of an event can happen at any time with no indication that it is about to occur. A Black Swan is a type of risk that is extraordinarily uncommon, carries harsh and widespread repercussions, and is regarded as obvious when looking back upon the event in retrospect[178]. No one expected for Ethereum to drop over 50%, which had major consequences for the ecosystem. Additionally, the mass liquidations that took place and the ability of someone to come in and exact a major windfall during the auction process was the unforeseen event everyone thought should have been addressed before Black Thursday occurred. Black Swans don't happen much but come with the territory of investments generally. It is a healthy reminder to never put all your eggs in one basket, and to diversify across several asset classes.

YAM

Early August 2020 saw the release of the YAM protocol that enabled yield farming for its users where the YAM token would keep uniformity with the dollar through a rebasing mechanism that expands and contracts the token supply[179]. YAM was the talk of DeFi when it hit the scene and was able to exceed over $600 million in Total Value Locked (TVL) in less than 36 hours after the commencement of the project. Not shortly after launch, an exploit in the rebasing smart contract was discovered that caused an excess of YAM tokens to be generated and were subsequently locked into the protocol reserve making the governance of the token useless. Despite catching the bug quickly, the development team's proposal to save the $750,000 in funds proved ultimately to have been insurmountable[180]. The price of YAM tokens topped $165 and fell to $0 after all was said and done. The mistake made leading to this failure was that the development team decided not to have the protocol's smart contracts audited. Such a mistake is an example of the technical risk DeFi users face when smart contracts are not properly audited. Before making a significant position on a protocol, be sure to ask the team if their smart contracts have undergone a third party audit.

SUSHI

A "rug pull" is a type of exit scam where a project that has adequate liquidity removes it and cashes out along the way, leaving the other liquidity providers and traders to scramble over what is left[181]. Rug pulls represent a type of financial/liquidity risk that are relatively prevalent in

2020, but there was one in particular that is worth discussing. Also in August of 2020, a copy of the UniSwap decentralized exchange and automated market maker (AMM) operating under the moniker of "SushiSwap" with its native Sushi token launched to much of the DeFi community's praise and fanfare. The lead developer went under the alias of "Chef Nomi" coupled with an avatar fashioned as a culinary panda bear. UniSwap works by supplanting the conventional order book of centralized exchanges with pools of tokens, thereby guaranteeing the liquidity to facilitate trades. Participants in these token pools are called Liquidity Providers or (LPs), and they are rewarded with a percentage of the fees earned in each trade. The goal of SushiSwap was to improve this process by creating a community-based token (SUSHI) that would be distributed among LPs along with the fees[182].

TVL in UniSwap leading to the SushiSwap migration was approaching $1.8 billion. The announcement of this UniSwap clone and their plan to migrate away from UniSwap with the liquidity it had injected onto the new more community-oriented DEX/AMM was lauded as genius, and the money pouring in was a testament of how much people did not want to miss out on what was the next big thing in DeFi[183]. After a successful migration, the SUSHI token was valued at just under $11 and Chef Nomi thought it was time to cash in and ride off into the sunset by cashing out his share of the 10% of tokens allocated to the development team, amounting to approximately $14 million, and passing ownership of the project to the CEO of the centralized FTX cryptocurrency exchange, Sam Bankman-Fried.

This rocked the confidence of the Sushi community in one regard that the DeFi project was selling out to a centralized exchange.

Additionally, the community was outraged and accused Nomi of perpetrating a rug pull. The Sushi price took a dive from $9.50 to $1.13 in five days after this move, which eventually saw Nomi apologize and return the 38,000 Ether drained from the project[184] [185]. Afterwards, SushiSwap imposed governance measures that included nine multi-signature wallet signers to ensure unilateral decisions are not made when it comes to funds and other improved voting protocols that have served to stabilize the price of the governance token[186]. What's notable about this instance was that it did not appear that Chef Nomi set out to develop and raise money for SushiSwap with the intention of scamming anyone. However, the success of the protocol may have activated Nomi's greed and he felt as though he was taking what he was owed. Nonetheless, cashing out completely and turning his back on the people who supported the project left people without many conclusions to come to other than Nomi pulled the rug out from under them.

Hacks

The single most prominent risk facing the DeFi ecosystem is cybersecurity risk. Cybersecurity risk represents a type of procedural/operational risk. Half of 2020's cryptocurrency thefts via cybersecurity exploits took place on DeFi protocols and exchanges. Total hacked volume from DeFi in 2020 came in at close to $100 million dollars[187] [188]. This is an indication of many things, but chief among them is that anyone seeking to utilize DeFi as a means of investment must take necessary precautions on their side with their devices and network security. Another good rule of thumb is to review the DeFi protocols to which you plan to pledge assets in order to assess the security risks that are present within a given project.

Chapter 12

THE THREAT

After the emancipation of slavery in the United States, Black Americans needed a place to store their funds as they were now able to make money for their labor, receive payment for their military service, and otherwise begin their greater engagement in American economic society. Realizing this, influential political and business leaders proposed Congress enact legislation around this concept. On March 3, 1865, Abraham Lincoln signed the Freedman's Bank Act that established a national bank for the newly emancipated former slaves[189]. The first president of the Freedman's Savings Bank was a Yankee named John W. Alvord, who undertook considerable outreach efforts to recruit Black soldiers on the orders of General Oliver Otis Howard that said, "...Negro soldiers should deposit their bounty money" with Alvord[190]. General Howard was highly revered by Black soldiers and former slaves for his accomplishments on the battlefield leading Union troops during the Civil War, his advocacy as a Commissioner in the Freedman's Bureau, and whose namesake is linked to the first Historically Black University[191]. In less than ten years from the signing of this law, the Freedman's Savings Bank saw considerable expansion with thirty-four branches throughout the country in cities like

New York, Atlanta, Memphis, Philadelphia, and Washington D.C. Alvord's aggressive mobilization campaign in 1865 was able to garner deposits equaling $3,299,201 or $77,429,916.51[1] when adjusted for today's dollars[192].

The turning point for the Freedman's Savings Banks was in 1871, when Congress allowed the bank to extend mortgages and business loans. However, when the majority of these business loans and mortgages were granted to Whites, who already had access to their own banks and financial institutions, gossip began to spread of the possibility that the White managers of the Freedman's Bank were perpetrating a fraud on its Black depositors. These anecdotes put pressure on the managers to mitigate the claims of corruption, so they decided to act quickly by installing a number of Black figureheads as insulation amid the growing concerns. Most notably, in March of 1874, Frederick Douglas was chosen to be the head of the bank[193]. By June 28, 1874, the Freedman's bank closed amid the scandal with 38% of the deposits never to be returned to their rightful owners. Frederick Douglas likened his short tenure with the bank akin to unknowingly being "marred to a corpse." Even WEB DuBois and Booker T Washington agreed on the notion that the bank's failure served to undermine the faith and livelihood of Black depositors who entrusted their funds with the Freedman's Bank[194].

It did not take the scholarly mind of Lincoln to appreciate the assumption that newly freed Black people needed a place to store, save,

---

[1] *https://www.measuringworth.com/dollarvaluetoday/?amount=3299201&from=1874*

and send their money as they migrated through the country. However, it was particularly sinister that a plan was devised at some level to manipulate the trust of free Black people in order to divest them of their newly gained opportunity to have and hold money after generations of themselves being bought and sold as commodities. The disdain for Black collective wealth has been a mainstay in modern history, whether we are talking about the story of the Freedman's Savings Bank or other great financial betrayals like the Tulsa Massacre, Project Spear, and the subprime mortgage debacle. This being the case, is it any wonder that the idea of financial assets that are out of the reach of the sovereign state resonates so strongly with Black people?

The Black Bitcoin Buyout

Lately there has been a concerted effort to have more Black people buy into Bitcoin under the auspices that it can't be seized, that it allows people to be their own bank and all of the other great things about digital assets. One recent promotional device by the name of the #BlackBitcoinBuyout, billed itself as, "The Biggest Transfer of Black Wealth" scheduled for August 11, 2020[195]. Specifically, the Black Bitcoin Buyout was aimed to be a collective investment to demonstrate Black buying power and profit at the same time. It was predicated on placing buy pressure on Bitcoin to the point that it would raise the price by creating an unusual demand for the asset. Black people were directed to purchase a minimum of $5 of Bitcoin on or before August 11, 2020 with the easiest method to obtain the asset being through Cash App. Some messages touted during this promotional push put forward notions that it could start the next market up cycle, and "It's time to take our power back!"

On the same day of the #BlackBitcoinBuyout, the business intelligence company, Microstrategy acquired 21,454 in Bitcoin at a price of $250,000,000[196]. The logic behind the Black Bitcoin Buyout would lead one to believe that MicroStrategy's quarter billion-dollar procurement of Bitcoin, in concert with all of the Black people demanding it on the same day would only serve to amplify price pressure on the asset and send prices through the roof. However, when analyzing the twenty-four-hour price movement on August 11, 2020, Bitcoin started the day off at $11,755.74 and actually dropped to $11,339.76 by the end of the day[197]. What is worse is when price is analyzed over a thirty-day period, the price of Bitcoin decreased by 8.7% to $10,355.75[198]. How is a newcomer to feel after being persuaded to invest in something new that came with so many promises only to end up coming up short? Granted, by the time of the publishing of this book market conditions for Bitcoin have improved handsomely, but what if some people were looking only to receive a short-term gain by this feat? Now that people who took part in this mass purchase event, what collective action should now be taken next to benefit the community as a whole? As much as this was an opportunity for people to profit, it also presented the opportunity for others to negatively impact the price like the short squeeze that took place with the video game retailer, GameStop[199].

The Black Bitcoin Buyout presents shades of the Freedman's Savings Bank in a few ways. First, like the Freedman's Bank scenario, there was a concerted outreach effort to target Black people's money.

Despite not knowing who the modern-day John Alvord is, it did seem clear that all of the Black social media influencers and participants lauding "The Biggest Transfer of Black Wealth" played the part of the modern day Frederick Douglas. This is not said to be disparaging to anyone who propagated this message, because they did so with the best of intentions, not fully realizing that this transfer of Black wealth that took place did nothing to benefit Black people. In fact, the people who bought into the Black Bitcoin Buyout suffered a loss of money like many of the Freedmen and Freedwomen after the initial thirty-day period. Secondly, there was a call to action much in the way that General Howard gave his troops and former slaves the order to make deposits with the Freedman's Savings Bank. Black people during the Black Bitcoin Buyout were prompted to "…take our power back" by illustrating our buying power and investing at least $5 on Cash App.

Cash App was mentioned several times in this campaign as the fastest way to obtain Bitcoin. Cash App is a mobile application that allows people to send and receive money in a peer-to-peer fashion[200]. Cash App is a subsidiary of the San Francisco based company Square, Inc. In the second quarter of 2020, Square reported $875 million dollars in revenue attributed to an increase in Bitcoin activities and growth in customer demand[201]. The CEO of Square is Jack Dorsey, who is also the CEO of Twitter. Isn't it coincidental that the person who owns the social media company that has the highest activity for this particular hashtag, also happens to own the payment processing company that is recommended in the campaign for Black people to make their Bitcoin purchases with? In no way is this meant to be an accusation towards Mr. Dorsey. Instead, it underscores the fact that although this was an event meant to improve the financial wellbeing of Black people, in the end, this transfer of Black wealth benefited a White man's companies through the ad traffic on Twitter and the fees generated on Cash App when the Bitcoin was purchased.

Another way the Black Bitcoin Buyout resembled the Freedman's Bank debacle is that it serves as a chilling effect to dissuade Black people from blockchain and the adoption of other cryptocurrencies. The Freedman's Savings Bank scandal served not only to cripple the trust of Freedmen and Freedwomen when it came to knowing who they could depend on when it came to safeguarding their money, it also financially wounded all the people who did not receive all or portions of their deposits back. Imagine the feeling of anyone in that position who suffered under enslavement, to experience emancipation and be free to earn a living, only to have the money you worked for be taken away. When looking at the Freedmen's Savings Bank case with the events of today, the COVID-19 pandemic has made Black people's ability to find jobs and earn a livelihood harder than it was prior to the shutdowns of businesses due to public safety concerns in the wake of the Coronavirus. In effect, losing money at that time would have served as an insult to injury, albeit at a lesser degree to those who lost money after the Freedman's Savings Bank collapse.

The good thing about the Black Bitcoin Buyout is that it serves as a lesson of what doesn't work. The worst part about this event was that it was incredibly shortsighted. There should have been more guidance and support as to what people should do in case Bitcoin price were to go south other than "hold!" Another supportive activity would be to show how the folks that bought in could properly secure their Bitcoin on their own wallets as opposed to Cash App's custodial account. Taking things further, it would have been great to see them organize a list of Black-owned businesses that accept Bitcoin and facilitate cooperative economics.

In the history of America, $331 billion has been lost as a result of discrimination related to lack of access to education, employment, and the denial of home loans to Black Americans. The American economy has forfeited roughly $13 trillion dollars because of not extending capital to Black-owned businesses. If this anti-Black discrimination were to somehow be remedied today, the United States could recapture $5 trillion in gross domestic productivity, but if history is a guide, there is not a strong possibility of this happening[202]. When examining these jarring figures, we as a community do not have time for games and promotional maneuvers. The everlasting threat of financial inequality has beaten us down for so long that it has kept us by and large in a survival mentality. This survival mentality has us falling for quick fix gimmicks in the hopes that someday we will be able to wake up, check the price of Bitcoin and our financial problems will disappear. Continuing down the path we are on and relying on the state, the legacy financial system, or Bitcoin to correct our collective economic suffering is almost a lost cause.

It is time to counter these state sanctioned practices with more focus and foresight because what is most under threat are the futures of the next generation of Black people that will be forced into economic devastation. If a meaningful number of us take the time now to dedicate the time and resources towards averting this tragedy, there is a chance that we can provide them with greater fiscal self-determination. We still have time to begin laying the groundwork of strategies and tactics to provide them with opportunities our ancestors never had. It is time to make the choice to begin moving away from reign of the legacy financial system towards an autonomous decentralized regime of programmable self-determination and self-sufficiency.

Chapter 13

THE CHOICE

T hrough the course of this book, there have been instances presented of open White supremacy operating in connection with the Bitcoin blockchain and several accounts and statistics of how traditional finance has operated in a covert manner to undermine our community's economic interests with the state either acting in concert with these participants or turning a blind eye. Black America and the global Black Diaspora are standing at a crossroads of a severe racial wealth gap, while simultaneously standing on the edge of a technological chasm that will only widen further if the proper measures are not taken to address these deficiencies. In 2016, the net worth of an average White household was ten times more than the average Black household. The space between White family wealth and the wealth of Black families is greater today than what it was twenty years ago, which means the gap is not closing but widening[203] [204]. Structural and infrastructural disparities have rendered Blacks 10 years behind Whites when it comes to broadband internet access. When Blacks are able to connect to the internet, they are four times more likely to have connectivity issues. According to a study on the racial wealth gap, 76% of Blacks will be underprepared for 86% of the jobs in the United States in 2045[205].

When examining the progression of the World Wide Web, although our community is able to utilize the Web, we as a collective have not have been able to benefit from it as much as we are consumers of it. Web 1.0 introduced us to internet browsers and email; unfortunately, Black people as a collective did very little to leverage it to our financial advantage. The same is true with where we are currently under Web 2.0 and social media. We are users, consumers, and creators of the content on these networks, but there is extraordinarily little ownership of these platforms and software applications that profit from our creativity and culture, while simultaneously censoring us and purveying historical stereotypes. In this way, our interaction with the web so far has become another zero-sum game.

The next step in the evolution of the internet bringing us to Web 3.0 will be regarded as a "Spatial Web." This means that the information flowing through the internet will now be integrated into our physical world. There will be a confluence of permissive technologies including 5G, IoT, artificial intelligence/machine learning (AI/ML), augmented and virtual reality (AR/VR), wearable technology, and blockchain/DLT[206]. According to a LinkedIn study, blockchain is 2020's hottest in demand skill. Blockchain will become integral in Web 3.0, which will be heralded by the fourth industrial revolution[207]. What's important to know about this fourth industrial revolution is with the emergence of artificial intelligence (AI), machine learning (ML), and the internet of things (IOT), blockchain will be integral in tying some of these other sectors together[208].

As Web 3.0 begins to emerge, we need to take this opportunity to invest in ourselves to close these gaps. The internet has done so much to make our world smaller and provide us with the ability to unite like never before, and blockchain will play a major factor in Web 3.0 with distributed ledger technology having the ability to drastically level the playing field. Blockchain can finally allow us more control over our content and the ability to create a more financially equitable ecosystem that can create virtuous cyclical benefits and begin moving away from the zero-sum games currently presented to us through legacy finance and certain crypto projects. DeFi serves as the major catalyst to facilitate improved group economics with little or no reliance on the traditional financial system. Presently, there is a cognitive dissonance that is separating us from what we know is holding us back as a cumulative financial entity and what we need to do to correct it. So the question now is, what will be the catalyst to take a critical mass of us from where we are now, to working in a more economically collaborative way? What is going to be the financial awakening that needs to take place equivalent to that of George Floyd, Breonna Taylor, Armaud Abury, Atatiana Jefferson, Tamir Rice, Sandra Bland, Trevon Martin, Aiyana Stanley-Jones, Oscar Grant, or any other name of a Black person lost at the hands of anti-Black violence? There are many strategic steps that can be taken in our approach towards semi-autonomous financial sovereignty, but the path to be proposed in the rest of this text will detail what we can do in the immediate future while working with a limited sector of legacy finance. We still need to proceed in a pragmatic fashion to ensure we can do things like pay bills, buy goods, and access the services needed to live comfortably.

Instead of fully investing in Bitcoin and other blockchain networks, my suggestion would be to infuse a portion of our capital and resources into projects and protocols that will allow the global Black collective to have more control over our financial outcomes. At the very least, we should know all or as many of the Black-owned or Black-focused blockchain projects out there and begin engaging. Beyond this, we should also embark upon approaching blockchain technology in several ways to ensure a heightened sense of financial self-determination. We can do this by identifying and segmenting people in a few categories before moving forward. Those categories are:

Group 1: Black people who have never been apprised of blockchain technology.

Group 2: Black people who are investors in blockchain/cryptocurrency projects.

Group 3: Black technology professionals who work on blockchain projects and people in the community that work in the information technology field.

Group 4: Black professionals who work in legacy/traditional finance.

The most important thing to do with Group 1 is direct them to verifiable information. The internet is rampant with misinformation on blockchain and digital assets. There is a plethora of existing Bitcoin and cryptocurrency related fraud schemes with the same patterns that continue to play themselves with new branding along with recent novel grifts coming out every day. Once this group of people begins to become exposed to blockchain, depending on their level of interest, they need to be directed towards three tracks:

A Track: Identifying the people who are most drawn towards the technical aspects of blockchain and begin educating and training them for the jobs of tomorrow that will enrich themselves and our community.

B Track: People who are the most interested in the financial aspect of cryptocurrencies and begin training them on financial literacy, how to trade, and the more complex areas of finance.

C Track: The last group will want nothing to do with either the technology or finance piece. This is okay because at the very least, they have been exposed to the subject matter and can begin thinking about how blockchain will eventually interface with the profession they will eventually choose and how they can use it to maximize their financial outcomes.

Black investors in blockchain projects (Group 2) around the world should come together to share information with one another, so that we can identify and assist the projects that have the best opportunity to succeed and mitigate our collective struggle. The proposition for Black programmers and other Black professionals working in technology sector (Group 3) is to assist with training the first group of people mentioned in the A Track, so that we do not have to rely on others outside of our community to continue to create financial technology solutions that don't have our best interests at heart. It is so important to begin educating this generation on blockchain technology like it was last year and not yesterday. We can't allow this financial paradigm shift to pass us by and once again be shut out and beholden to the same forces that have pushed the same predatory and exclusionary practices upon us as before.

When it comes to the Black financial professionals in Group 4, I believe that there can be a concerted effort made to work within a small group within traditional finance to assist in crafting the tools that will allow us to loosen the grip this industry has had over our community for generations. It is imperative to begin building bridges with them and other blockchain professionals. A brain trust between Black financial professionals and Black blockchain professionals ensures mistakes can be avoided that have the ability to compromise the vision of what is possible. Leveraging the people within our community that have the institutional knowledge and wisdom to assist in building this new era of Black sustainability on both fronts will also speed the pace of progress. Many people involved in cryptocurrencies historically have taken a position of "F_(orget?) the banks." This perspective is understandable since non-Black-owned banks have a clearly documented history of exclusion. Less than 1% of mortgages at non-Black-owned banks go to Black Americans; however, Black-owned banks issue 67% of their mortgage loans to Black homebuyers[209]. It is naïve to take the stance that we will not need to use banks for the foreseeable future to take care of commitments like paying bills, check cashing, and the services necessary to function with relative ease when it comes to our finances. Also, it should not be unreasonable to begin making dedicated efforts toward being more supportive of Black banks that are willing to provide us with access to capital within centralized finance. Why not support the Black banks that have fought hard to survive through generations to provide services to our community in a manner that has been equitable and accommodating? Every Black household in America should strive to switch to a Black bank within the next two to four years. It is not asking much to take the time to open an account (which can be done online or over the phone), even if it is for the purposes of savings. This approach will allow us to give greater support to the Black-owned banks that support us and allow them to strengthen within traditional finance.

According to new guidance from the U.S. Department of Treasury's Office of the Comptroller of the Currency (OCC), banks are now able to take custody of clients' digital assets[210]. What this means is Black banks can provide custodial services of cryptocurrencies to safeguard customers' holdings in the event of a family tragedy that would allow successors to have their decedents' digital assets passed to them. This service would minimize the possibility of Black generational wealth being lost if a family member with digital assets passes away and their private keys are unable to be accessed. More recent guidance from the OCC and the Securities and Exchange Commission has clarified the ability of banks to carry stablecoin reserves on behalf of their issuers[211]. Now that there is requisite guidance in place for banks to handle custody of digital assets and fiat-backed stablecoins, it is time for Black banks to begin offering these services to the community. This will allow Black banks to add new lines of business to strengthen their ability to grow and innovate in this new era of financial technology while simultaneously protecting their Black customers who invest in digital assets.

While we are furnishing this support to our Black banks operating within traditional finance, the creation of a community bank that operates as a voluntary, sustainable, permissionless, decentralized financial engine that manages several smart contracts to allow participants to be rewarded in dividends of digital currency is something that should also be pursued[212]. Part of the smart contract fees for participants can go toward things like an educational fund to ensure young people in the Diaspora have access to the science, technology, engineering, and math programs; a food stability fund that supports Black farmers and ensures participants in their region receive healthy provisions; a political fund that supports and cultivates politicians with an authentic Black agenda; a housing fund that pursues real estate development and seeks to alleviate Black homelessness; an arts and culture fund that ensures that there are no starving artists in our community that are subject to corporate interests, which may stymie true creative vision; and several other scenarios that are all possible through DeFi.

If the right people are able to come together in the aforementioned groups and create decentralized financial networks, protocols and assets founded upon the principles and morals our community needs, we can do even more things like fund mortgages and small business loans when traditional financial institutions won't; provide short-term lending at reasonable interest rates so that predatory lending in our communities becomes a thing of the past; assist in crafting and funding insurance and the bonding products Black businesses need to be eligible for government and other capital contracts; and create systems so that people of African heritage, no matter where they are in the world, can build wealth and provide a basic income. As a result, more of our needs will be met and funds can go toward the institutions that will ensure self-determination for years into perpetuity.

This may sound ambitious but what is the alternative? Wait as the wealth gap between us and the rest of the world widens? Remain in a system that will continue to leverage our talents, culture, and resources to ensure we remain a financial pariah? Proceeding down the road we have been on only leads to an existence where we continue to compete with one another for financial resources instead of competing with the rest of the world.

The choice is ours.

Acknowledgements

Kairin Hubbard, I had you in mind when writing this book and hope that the information within this text can help you at some point in life. Julianne Malveaux, Claude Anderson, and Boyce Watkins for being role models for the Black community in the areas of finance and economics. Bryce Weiner Thanks for the opportunity to learn with you and learn from you on my journey towards better understanding blockchain and DLT. Gwen Freeman, Ph.D., thank you for your early editorial assistance with my manuscript. Paul Viotti, Ph.D. thanks for the recommendations for some of historical economic illustrations for this book.

About the Author

Kamal Hubbard is a lawyer by training who spent several years at Stanford University's Rock Center for Corporate Governance, a collaboration between the Graduate School of Business and Stanford Law School. While there, he worked with a former Securities and Exchange Commissioner and managed research into federal securities litigation and global corruption. Kamal is certified in Fraud Examination, Cybersecurity, and Decentralized Finance. Kamal spent two years (2013-2015) conducting individual research on Bitcoin and blockchain technology before entering a position in cryptocurrencies. He is a civil rights officer; the founder of the blockchain consulting company, CageChain Media Group; co-founder of FanMix, LLC; serves as an advisor to the Tao Network Blockchain, and sits on the Board of the North Hollywood based AltMarket Cryptocurrency Exchange. In 2018, he had the privilege of testifying before California's Senate Banking Committee on the basics of blockchain and Bitcoin. Kamal also served as part of the Blockchain Advocacy Coalition in support of California bills AB 2658 and SB 838, which provided a definition of "blockchain" under California state law and allowed businesses to transfer equity using distributed ledgers. Kamal has also participated in discussions with the US Department of the Treasury's Office of the Comptroller of the Currency on matters related to the intersection of cryptocurrencies and banking.

References:

[1] Scott Ellsworth, *Death in a Promised Land*: *The Tulsa Race Riot of 1921*, (Louisiana State University, 1982); History and Political Science at Montgomery College. *The Tulsa Race Riot of 1921*.
https://www.blackpast.org/african-american-history/tulsa-race-riot-1921/
[2] https://showme.co.za/lifestyle/on-a-mission/
[3] https://www.cbsnews.com/news/redlining-what-is-history-mike-bloomberg-comments/
[4] Ibid
[5] https://www.mckinsey.com/industries/financial-services/our-insights/counting-the-worlds-unbanked#
[6] https://www.investopedia.com/terms/b/bitcoin-maximalism.asp
[7] https://www.urban.org/urban-wire/these-five-facts-reveal-current-crisis-black-homeownership
[8] https://www.forbes.com/sites/haileylennon/2020/07/22/bitcoin-meets-banking-as-us-bank-regulator-permits-cryptocurrency-custody/#5c81445479ba
[9] https://regardnews.com/could-this-racist-person-be-a-real-satoshi-nakamoto/
[10] https://twitter.com/nickszabo4
[11] https://www.coindesk.com/people/nick-szabo
[12] https://www.businessinsider.com/iq-tests-dark-history-finally-being-used-for-good-2017-10?op=1
[13] https://www.mic.com/articles/186438/neo-nazi-wealth-is-rapidly-growing-why-bitcoin
[14] https://twitter.com/NeonaziWallets
[15] https://cryptobriefing.com/unmasking-deceased-programmer-donated-bitcoin-capitol-hill-rioters/
[16] http://btcbase.org/log/2013-08-11
[17] https://cryptobriefing.com/unmasking-deceased-programmer-donated-bitcoin-capitol-hill-rioters/
[18] https://blog.chainalysis.com/reports/capitol-riot-bitcoin-donation-alt-right-domestic-extremism
[19] https://www.nbcnews.com/politics/immigration/white-nationalist-leader-plotting-take-over-gop-n920826
[20] https://www.adl.org/education/references/hate-symbols/american-identity-movement-aim
[21] https://www.independent.co.uk/news/uk/politics/david-irving-holocaust-denial-neo-nazi-alt-right-london-forum-meeting-auschwitz-hitler-revisionist-a7719291.html
[22] https://www.splcenter.org/hatewatch/2020/11/17/extremists-are-cashing-youth-targeted-gaming-website
[23] https://blog.chainalysis.com/reports/capitol-riot-bitcoin-donation-alt-right-domestic-extremism
[24] https://thetab.com/us/bu/2017/08/22/theres-a-leaked-video-of-nick-fuentes-making-more-racist-and-anti-semitic-comments-13124
[25] https://twitter.com/ReaganBattalion/status/894009774634930176
[26] https://twitter.com/NickJFuentes/status/1340196694571540490
[27] https://www.pbs.org/wgbh/frontline/article/several-well-known-hate-groups-identified-at-capitol-riot/
[28] https://twitter.com/MeganSquire0/status/1346478478523125767
[29] https://twitter.com/NickJFuentes/status/1346978532837056515

30 https://www.hngn.com/articles/230746/20200721/two-italian-teens-pay-bitcoins-watch-livestream-children-being-tortured.htm

31 https://www.ilmessaggero.it/italia/deep_web_dark_web_red_room_cosa_sono_stanze_degli_orrori_17enni_pagavano_bimbi_uccisi_diretta-5347921.html

32 https://www.hngn.com/articles/230746/20200721/two-italian-teens-pay-bitcoins-watch-livestream-children-being-tortured.htm

33

https://www.law.umich.edu/special/exoneration/Documents/Race_and_Wrongful_Convictions.pdf

34 https://www.investopedia.com/terms/m/money.asp

35 https://www.investopedia.com/ask/answers/052515/what-difference-between-banks-liquidity-and-its-liquid-assets.asp

36 https://www.investopedia.com/terms/m/mediumofexchange.asp

37 Yu, L., & Yu, H. (2004). Chinese coins: money in history and society (Vol. 7). Long River Press.

38 https://africa.si.edu/exhibits/site/cowrie.htm

39 Ibid

40 https://africa.si.edu/exhibits/site/kissi.htm

41 Ibid

42 https://africa.si.edu/exhibits/site/ingots.htm

43 McCulloch, J.R., 1858. A treatise on Metallic and Paper Money, and Banks. Written for the Encyclopædia Britannica.

44 Vogel, H.U., 2013. Marco Polo was in China: new evidence from currencies, salts and revenues. Brill.

45 Ages, M., 2015. COINAGE IN EUROPE. World Monarchies and Dynasties, p.196.

46 Granatstein, J.L., 2016. Canada 1957-1967: The years of uncertainty and innovation (Vol. 19). McClelland & Stewart.

47 https://www.investopedia.com/ask/answers/09/gold-standard.asp

48 Ibid

49 Ibid

50 https://www.federalreservehistory.org/essays/bretton_woods_created

51 https://www.investopedia.com/ask/answers/09/gold-standard.asp

52 https://www.federalreservehistory.org/essays/bretton_woods_created

53 https://www.investopedia.com/terms/b/brettonwoodsagreement.asp

54 https://www.federalreservehistory.org/essays/bretton_woods_created

55 https://www.investopedia.com/terms/b/brettonwoodsagreement.asp

56 https://www.merriam-webster.com/dictionary/fiat%20money

57 https://www.investopedia.com/terms/f/fiatmoney.asp

58 Ibid

59 https://www.yourfxcoach.com/what-is-the-daily-forex-trading-volume/

60 Jack, W. and Suri, T., 2011. Mobile money: The economics of M-PESA (No. w16721). National Bureau of Economic Research.

61 Gautam, A., 2019. Immutable Storage of EV Charge Records Using Blockchain Technology.

62 Michie, R.C., 1986. The London and New York Stock Exchanges, 1850-1914. Journal of Economic History, pp.171-187.

63 Sarr, A. and Lybek, T., 2002. Measuring liquidity in financial markets (Vol. 2). International Monetary Fund.

64 https://www.britannica.com/place/Weimar-Republic/The-Ruhr-and-inflation

[65] Ibid

[66] Ibid

[67] https://www.britannica.com/biography/Cecil-Rhodes

[68] https://www.dallasfed.org/~/media/documents/institute/annual/2011/annual11b.pdf

[69] https://www.britannica.com/biography/Ian-Smith

[70] Ibid

[71] https://www.economist.com/middle-east-and-africa/2009/03/05/whose-land

[72] Ibid

[73] https://en.wikipedia.org/wiki/Hyperinflation_in_Zimbabwe

[74] https://www.dallasfed.org/~/media/documents/institute/annual/2011/annual11b.pdf

[75] https://www.investopedia.com/terms/i/interestrate.asp

[76] https://corporatefinanceinstitute.com/resources/knowledge/other/per-annum/

[77] https://www.investopedia.com/terms/a/apr.asp

[78] https://www.investopedia.com/ask/answers/who-determines-interest-rates/

[79] https://www.bloombergquint.com/gadfly/egyptians-are-no-better-off-than-before-the-arab-spring

[80] Ibid

[81] https://archive.nytimes.com/www.nytimes.com/interactive/2013/07/02/world/middleeast/03egypt-timeline-morsi.html

[82] https://www.reuters.com/article/us-egypt-reserves/egypt-foreign-reserves-see-first-gain-since-2010-idUSBRE84508H20120506

[83] https://archive.nytimes.com/www.nytimes.com/interactive/2013/07/02/world/middleeast/03egypt-timeline-morsi.html

[84] https://www.bloombergquint.com/gadfly/egyptians-are-no-better-off-than-before-the-arab-spring

[85] https://archive.nytimes.com/www.nytimes.com/interactive/2013/07/02/world/middleeast/03egypt-timeline-morsi.html

[86] https://money.cnn.com/2016/08/11/news/economy/egypt-bailout-imf/?iid=EL

[87] https://www.investopedia.com/terms/e/egp.asp

[88] https://money.cnn.com/2016/11/03/news/economy/egypt-pound-devaluation-bailout/

[89] https://www.investopedia.com/terms/e/egp.asp

[90] https://www.frbatlanta.org/-/media/documents/research/publications/economic-review/1996/vol81no1_whitt.pdf

[91] https://www.investopedia.com/terms/b/businesscycle.asp

[92] https://www.investopedia.com/terms/g/great_depression.asp

[93] https://www.investopedia.com/terms/g/great-recession.asp

[94] https://www.aclu.org/files/field_document/discrimlend_final.pdf

[95] Ibid

[96] https://www.bls.gov/opub/mlr/2014/article/consumer-spending-and-us-employment-from-the-recession-through-2022.htm

[97] https://www.investopedia.com/ask/answers/100314/whats-difference-between-monetary-policy-and-fiscal-policy.asp

[98] https://www.investopedia.com/terms/q/quantitative-easing.asp

[99] Ibid

[100] https://www.investopedia.com/ask/answers/100314/whats-difference-between-monetary-policy-and-fiscal-policy.asp

[101] https://www.investopedia.com/terms/g/great-recession.asp

[102] https://www.investopedia.com/terms/a/american-recovery-and-reinvestment-act.asp

[103] https://www.investopedia.com/terms/q/quantitative-easing.asp

[104] https://thehill.com/policy/finance/531860-questions-and-answers-on-covid-relief-package-thats-now-law

[105] https://www.federalreserve.gov/econres/notes/feds-notes/disparities-in-wealth-by-race-and-ethnicity-in-the-2019-survey-of-consumer-finances-20200928.htm

[106] Swan, M., 2015. Blockchain: Blueprint for a new economy. "O'Reilly Media, Inc."

[107] https://crypto.stanford.edu/~dabo/cryptobook/BonehShoup_0_4.pdf

[108] http://practicalcryptography.com/ciphers/

[109] Underwood, S., 2016. Blockchain beyond bitcoin.

[110] Crosby, M., Pattanayak, P., Verma, S. and Kalyanaraman, V., 2016. Blockchain technology: Beyond bitcoin. Applied Innovation, 2(6-10), p.71.

[111] Drescher, D., 2017. Blockchain basics (Vol. 276). Berkeley, CA: Apress.

[112] Ibid

[113] https://blogs.cornell.edu/info4220/2013/03/29/bitcoin-and-the-double-spending-problem/

[114] https://academy.ivanontech.com/blog/byzantine-generals-problem-an-introduction

[115] http://pages.cs.wisc.edu/~sschang/OS-Qual/reliability/byzantine.htm

[116] https://academy.ivanontech.com/blog/byzantine-generals-problem-an-introduction

[117] https://www.exodus.io/blog/proof-of-work-vs-proof-of-stake/

[118] Ibid

[119] https://medium.com/@robertgreenfieldiv/explaining-proof-of-stake-f1eae6feb26f

[120] https://www.investopedia.com/terms/a/asic.asp

[121] https://blockchainengineer.com/centralized-vs-decentralized-vs-distributed-network/

[122] https://medium.com/nakamo-to/whats-the-difference-between-decentralized-and-distributed-1b8de5e7f5a4

[123] https://medium.com/distributed-economy/what-is-the-difference-between-decentralized-and-distributed-systems-f4190a5c6462

[124] https://www.investopedia.com/news/public-private-permissioned-blockchains-compared/

[125] https://cointelegraph.com/explained/crypto-wallets-explained

[126] https://cryptovoucher.io/bitcoin-wallets-differences-explained#

[127] Ibid

[128] Ibid

[129] Ibid

[130] Vujičić, D., Jagodić, D. and Ranđić, S., 2018, March. Blockchain technology, bitcoin, and Ethereum: A brief overview. In 2018 17th international symposium infoteh-jahorina (infoteh) (pp. 1-6). IEEE.

[131] Ibid

[132] https://www.bbc.com/news/business-47553048

[133] https://www.coingecko.com/en

[134] Ibid

[135] https://www.investopedia.com/terms/i/ipo.asp

[136] https://cryptonews.com/guides/countries-in-which-bitcoin-is-banned-or-legal.htm

[137] Ibid

[138] https://www.coindesk.com/ohio-becomes-first-us-state-to-allow-taxes-to-be-paid-in-bitcoin

[139] https://www.sec.gov/news/speech/peirce-remarks-blockress-2020-02-06

[140] https://coincenter.org/entry/sec-commissioner-proposes-safe-harbor-for-projects-that-raise-funds-to-build-decentralized-networks

[141] https://medium.com/@brucefenton/the-sec-blockchain-safe-harbor-proposal-cbeb66ce272a

[142] 328 U.S. 293 (1946)

[143] https://consumer.findlaw.com/securities-law/what-is-the-howey-test.html

[144] https://dcebrief.com/secs-hester-proposes-safe-harbor-for-decentralized-networks/

[145] Baldwin, Clare. 2020. "Bitcoin Worth $72 Million Stolen From Bitfinex Exchange In Hong Kong". U.S.. https://www.reuters.com/article/us-bitfinex-hacked-hongkong-idUSKCN10E0KP.

[146] Magas, Julia. 2020. "DEX, Explained". Cointelegraph. https://cointelegraph.com/explained/dex-explained

[147] Ibid

[148] https://blog.drhack.net/etherdelta-hacked-millions-stolen/

[149] Ibid

[150] https://www.forbes.com/sites/ericervin/2018/08/16/blockchain-technology-set-to-revolutionize-global-stock-trading/#77674a984e56

[151] Schär, Fabian. "Decentralized Finance: On Blockchain-and Smart Contract-based Financial Markets." Available at SSRN 3571335 (2020).

[152] Chen, Yan, and Cristiano Bellavitis. "Blockchain disruption and decentralized finance: The rise of decentralized business models." Journal of Business Venturing Insights 13 (2020): e00151.

[153] https://hackernoon.com/decentralized-and-trustless-networks-f881671fae4e

[154] https://www.investopedia.com/terms/s/smart-contracts.asp

[155] https://www.investopedia.com/news/daos-and-potential-ownerless-business/

[156] https://academy.ivanontech.com/blog/decentralized-money-markets-and-makerdao

[157] Ibid

[158] http://blockgeeks.com/guides/what-is-blockchain-governance-ultimate-beginners-guide

[159] https://www.coindesk.com/defi-yield-farming-comp-token-explained

[160] Ibid

[161] https://hackernoon.com/a-comprehensive-guide-to-decentralized-stablecoins-22f66553c807

[162] https://www.thebusinessresearchcompany.com/report/insurance-global-market-report-2018

[163] https://www.bbc.com/news/business-49476247

[164] https://medium.com/plutusdefi/risk-in-defi-part-1-3-procedural-hacks-and-how-to-avoid-them-72e7512a91e1

[165] Ibid

[166] https://www.investopedia.com/terms/d/derivative.asp

[167] https://www.investopedia.com/ask/answers/052715/how-big-derivatives-market.asp

[168] https://www.investopedia.com/terms/d/derivative.asp

[169] https://academy.ivanontech.com/blog/the-ultimate-guide-to-decentralized-finance-defi

[170] Chen, Yan, and Cristiano Bellavitis. "Blockchain disruption and decentralized finance: The rise of decentralized business models." Journal of Business Venturing Insights 13 (2020): e00151.
[171] https://www.bbc.com/news/business-47553048
[172] Chen, Yan. "Decentralized finance: Blockchain technology and the quest for an open financial system." Available at SSRN 3418557 (2019).
[173] Ibid
[174] https://www.forbes.com/sites/cryptoconfidential/2020/03/29/congress-flirts-with-digital-dollar-cryptos-hiring-boom/#1169bc9b2633
[175] https://mcusercontent.com/3bcee1ef2023cd3e45524e325/files/8671fb2b-9c37-451d-87c1-12d97f88b396/BNC_Research_Identifying_Key_Non_Financial_Risks_in_DeFi_on_Ethereum_Blockchain.pdf
[176] https://cointelegraph.com/news/30m-makerdao-black-thursday-lawsuit-sent-to-arbitration
[177] https://cointelegraph.com/news/maker-debt-crisis-post-mortem-recommends-new-safeguards
[178] https://www.investopedia.com/terms/b/blackswan.asp
[179] https://www.coindesk.com/yams-market-cap-falls-from-60m-to-zero-in-35-minutes
[180] https://defirate.com/yam-finance-post-mortem/
[181] https://www.coingecko.com/en/glossary/rug-pulled
[182] https://decrypt.co/41236/sushiswap-what-happened-what-it-means-for-defi-and-whats-next
[183] https://decrypt.co/41236/sushiswap-what-happened-what-it-means-for-defi-and-whats-next
[184] https://cointelegraph.com/news/chef-nomi-has-returned-all-funds-back-to-the-sushiswap-community
[185] https://www.coindesk.com/sushiswap-creator-chef-nomi-returns-dev-fund
[186] https://www.coindesk.com/sushiswap-migration-defi-protocol-politicians
[187] https://ciphertrace.com/half-of-2020-crypto-hacks-are-from-defi-protocols-and-exchanges/
[188] https://www.supercryptonews.com/defi-protocol-attacks-have-resulted-in-losses-of-100-million/
[189] https://www.occ.treas.gov/about/who-we-are/history/1863-1865/1863-1865-freedmans-savings-bank.html
[190] https://theconversation.com/22-million-reasons-black-america-doesnt-trust-banks-37982
[191] https://www.britannica.com/biography/Oliver-O-Howard
[192] https://theconversation.com/22-million-reasons-black-america-doesnt-trust-banks-37982
[193] https://www.occ.treas.gov/about/who-we-are/history/1863-1865/1863-1865-freedmans-savings-bank.html
[194] https://theconversation.com/22-million-reasons-black-america-doesnt-trust-banks-37982
[195] https://twitter.com/search?q=%23blackbtcbuyout
[196] https://news.bitcoin.com/billion-dollar-public-company-microstrategy-250-million-btc-bitcoin-superior-to-cash/
[197] https://www.coingecko.com/en/coins/bitcoin
[198] Ibid

[199] https://www.npr.org/2021/01/27/961291455/gamestop-and-the-short-squeeze
[200] https://www.nerdwallet.com/blog/banking/cash-app-peer-to-peer-money-transfer-service/
[201] https://news.bitcoin.com/square-cash-app-bitcoin-revenue-surges-600-875-million-q2-profit-up-711/
[202] https://www.cbsnews.com/news/us-gdp-growth-missed-16-trillion-systemic-racism-inequality-report/
[203] https://www.brookings.edu/blog/up-front/2020/02/27/examining-the-black-white-wealth-gap/
[204] https://www.demos.org/sites/default/files/publications/RacialWealthGap_1.pdf
[205] https://www.dbresearch.com/PROD/RPS_EN-PROD/PROD0000000000511664/America%27s_Racial_Gap_%26_Big_Tech%27s_Closing_Window.pdf
[206] https://www2.deloitte.com/us/en/insights/topics/digital-transformation/web-3-0-technologies-in-business.html
[207] https://theblockchainland.com/2020/01/15/linkedin-blockchain-2020-hottest-skill/
[208] Ibid
[209] https://www.nerdwallet.com/blog/banking/black-owned-banks-fight-to-bounce-back/
[210] https://www.occ.gov/news-issuances/news-releases/2020/nr-occ-2020-98.html
[211] https://www.coindesk.com/wp-content/uploads/2020/09/Federally-Chartered-Banks-and-Thrifts-May-Engage-in-Certain-Stablecoin-Activities.pdf
[212] https://bankroll.network/media/bankroll-whitepaper.pdf

CPSIA information can be obtained
at www.ICGtesting.com
Printed in the USA
BVHW090322070521
606654BV00007B/1097